STUDY SKILLS
FOR STUDENTS
IN OUR SCHOOLS

Stephen B. McCarney, Ed.D.
Janet K. Tucci, M.Ed.

Copyright © 1991 by Hawthorne Educational Services Inc.

Printed in the
United States of America

Hawthorne
Educational Services Inc.
800 Gray Oak Drive
Columbia, Missouri 65201
Telephone: (314) 874-1710

Table of Contents

B. Academic Behavior

Behavior
Number

C. Math Skills

Behavior
Number

D. Language Arts Skills

Behavior
Number

E. Reading Skills

Behavior
Number

I. Introduction

The increased learning and behavior problems that are being encountered by educators in our schools are the result of the changing nature of our society. We are seeing an increased number of students being referred to as "At-Risk" as well as an increased number of problems encountered by the students we refer to as "typical" or "average."

By anyone's perception, it must be recognized that the number of students we consider "At-Risk" is increasing at an alarming pace. In 1989 the poverty rate was 13.1%, indicating that one in eight Americans live at the poverty level. More than 12.6 million U.S. youngsters, nearly 20% of all children under the age of 18, are poor. Thus, one in five American children goes to bed hungry or sick or cold (Reed & Sautter, 1990), and the future seems even grimmer. Former Secretary of Education Lauro Cavazos has estimated that, by the year 2000, "as many as one-third of our young people will be disadvantaged and 'At-Risk'" (Reed & Sautter, 1990). If a child lives in a family headed by a woman, the chances are better than 50/50 that the child is poor (Reed & Sautter, 1990). In our country 222,000 children are homeless, and of that 222,000; 65,000 do not attend school.

At least half of all the children in our schools are faced with family divorce or separation before they are 18 years old. At least 1 million children a year are victims of child abuse and/or neglect, an increase of two-thirds over 1980 estimates. The dropout rate among students who begin the ninth grade and do not finish high school is 25%. Reports in some metropolitan areas are even more drastic. For example, Chicago, Boston, Detroit, and Los Angeles school officials estimate that between 40% and 60% of their students drop out. Girls between the ages of 10 and 17 years of age make up 31% of the pregnant population. Five hundred suicide attempts are made every day among students ranging in age from 15-19 years old.

These figures suggest that the student who is considered "At-Risk" is rapidly leaving the status of minority and is becoming the majority of students in our schools.

It would seem an impossibility to define "At-Risk" in a manner that would satisfy all perceptions of the "At-Risk" dilemma. It is certain that "At-Risk" means different things to different people. To the teacher, "At-Risk" may mean the student is "At-Risk" for failure which which will result in eventual retention or quitting of school at the end of the year. To the social worker, "At-Risk" may mean that an abused child is "At-Risk" for becoming an abusive parent. To a social or economic analyst, an "At-Risk" child is one who is born out of wedlock, grows up in poverty and is likely to repeat the cycle.

Study Skills for Students In Our Schools was developed in response to requests for intervention strategies for the most common learning problems encountered by regular educators in their classrooms in meeting the needs of "At-Risk" students. The study skills contained in the guide for the learning problems identified are those that regular education personnel have found most effective with the "At-Risk" student in need of more success in regular education classrooms. A wide variety of study skills interventions are provided for each learning problem contained in the guide. The variety of interventions allows the educators involved in teaching to choose the study skills interventions most likely to contribute to each individual student's success. A primary expectation is that much more consistency of instructional intervention will be attained when the guide is used to find a common set of interventions which contribute to the individual student's success. This consistency of study skills interventions on the part of all teachers working with the student is likely to markedly enhance student success.

This guide offers teachers various ways to improve the study skills of students who are "At-Risk" and, at the same time, improve the study skills for all students. Contained herein is an individualized program designed to meet the needs of those students who are slipping between the cracks or, of greater concern, those students who will fail to develop the basic skills of learning in the school and post-school environment.

In the sophisticated school and post-school environment today, developing successful study skills is a must for any student. It is an absolute survival skill for the "At-Risk." While the study skills strategies contained in this guide apply particularly to "At-Risk" students, they are generally applicable to improving the academic success of all students in our schools.

This guide was developed to be implemented in coursework activities for grades K-12. The variety of intervention strategies suggested by the authors presents a selection of study skills which are appropriate for all ages and ability levels of students.

Thanks to all those educators who have shared strategies used to help their students succeed; and to all the teachers who face the insurmountable task of helping our students succeed, "God bless you."

Stephen B. McCarney, Ed.D.
Janet K. Tucci, M.Ed.

The data references were collected from the following sources:

"Bad-New Poverty Figures," *The Washington Post,* October 22, 1989, pp. C6.

Balch, P.,"Reducing Twenty-First Century Dropouts," *The Clearing House,* December 1989, pp. 170-171.

Mohler, M. (1987, November). Teen Suicide the Sobering Facts. *Ladies Home Journal,* 106.

Reed, S., & Sautter, C. (1990, June). "Children of Poverty, The Status of 12 Million Young Americans: Kappan Special Report," *Phi Delta Kappan,* June 1990, pp. K1-K11.

Rich, S. (1988, June 30), "Child Abuse and Neglect Up Sharply," *The Washington Post, June 30, 1988, p.* A66.

Vobejda, B, (1989, February 18) "220,000 School-Children Lack Homes, "*The Washington Post,* February 18, 1989, p. A7.

II. Using the Study Skills Guide

● The materials and strategies included herein were carefully designed to provide a systematic, easy approach to the complex process of learning. It was our intention to reduce the difficulty encountered by many students in the educational setting by providing teachers, parents and students with a systematic approach to learning how to learn.

● The following section contains sample materials and explanations of suggested use. We fully realize that those who are learning and teaching have individual styles and preferences. We encourage both the student and the teacher to search for the best match of method and content.

● In Section III, specific behavioral interventions are provided for teacher or parent use. Studying is a complex process, therefore we purport to reduce its complexity by breaking it down into manageable steps. Teachers and parents should choose interventions that will work for their student. Although several interventions can be implemented simultaneously, any intervention requires adequate trial time to determine its effectiveness.

Note Taking

1. For note taking from lecture or written material, follow:

    ● **Outline Form**
       (e.g., Who, What, Where, When, How, Why)

    ● **Mapping Form**
       (e.g., Who, What, Where, When, How, Why)

    ● **Double-Column Form**
       (e.g., Who, What, Where, When, How, Why)

2. For note taking from directions, follow:

    ● **Assignment Form**
       (e.g., What, How, Materials, When)

    ● **Assignment Sheet**

    ● **2-Week Project Outline**

✳ (See Appendix for the above forms.)

Suggestions for Note Taking

1. For note taking from lecture or written material:

    ● The Outline Form is a format for organizing information received through lecture or written material. The student is provided with a form that lists Who, What, Where, When, How, and Why. As information is delivered/read, the student answers the questions: Who, What, Where, When, How, and Why on the Outline Form. The student should be aware that information delivered/read may not conform to the order of the Outline Form. (See the sample of the Outline Form on a subsequent page. A copy of the Outline Form is included in the Appendix.)

    ● The Mapping Form is also a format for organizing information received through lecture or written material. A primary difference is that the Mapping Form requires the student to be more concise in note taking. The student is provided with a form with rectangles for recording Topic, Who, What, Where, When, How, and Why. As information is delivered/read, the student fills in the corresponding rectangles that answer the questions: Who, What, Where, When, How, and Why on the Mapping Form. (See the sample of the Mapping Form on a subsequent page. A copy of the Mapping Form is included in the Appendix.)

● The Double-Column Form is also a format for organizing information received through lecture or written material. The student is be provided with a form that lists Who, What, Where, When, How, and Why or the student may use a blank piece of paper to fold in half lengthwise. The student lists specific questions in the left column: Who, What, Where, When, How, and Why; and indicates the answers to these questions in the right column. Again, the student should be aware that information delivered/read may not conform to the order of the Double-Column Form. (See the sample of the Double-Column Form on a subsequent page. A copy of the Double-Column Form is included in the Appendix.)

2. For note taking from directions:

● The Assignment Form is a format for organizing oral directions given in the classroom for a single subject area. The student is provided with a form that lists What, How, Materials, and When. As information is delivered, the student completes the What, How, Materials, and When information for both General and Specific areas on the Assignment Form. The student should be aware that information delivered may not conform to the order of the Assignment Form. (See the sample of the Assignment Form on a subsequent page. A copy of the Assignment Form is included in the Appendix.)

● The Assignment Sheet is a format for recording assignments given in the classroom for all subject areas. Each day the student is provided with a form that lists all subject areas and has corresponding columns for Assignment, Due Date, and Teacher Signature. As information is received, the student fills in the corresponding Subject, Assignment and Due Date. The teacher signs to verify the accuracy of the assignment. (See the sample of the Assignment Sheet on a subsequent page. A copy of the Assignment Sheet is included in the Appendix.)

● The 2-Week Project Outline is a format for organizing and developing a class project. The student is provided with a form that lists suggested activities for Day 1 through Day 14 for completion of a project. The student completes the indicated steps with as much detail as possible. The student then follows the 2-Week Project Outline in completing his/her project. (See the sample of the 2-Week Project Outline on a subsequent page. A copy of the 2-Week Project Outline is included in the Appendix.)

✳ (See Appendix for the forms mentioned above.)

Paragraph Sample

THE SANTA FE TRAIL

In the 1820's, settlers began to move west in prairie schooners, or covered wagons, on the Santa Fe Trail. The Santa Fe Trail extended for about eight hundred miles from Independence, Missouri, to Santa Fe, New Mexico.

In 1812, Santa Fe was part of Mexico. The people who lived in Santa Fe needed supplies such as guns, mules, coffee, cloth and tools. Although these supplies were available in Mexico, Missouri's trading centers were closer. Therefore, the Santa Fe Trail became a trade route between Santa Fe and Independence.

Outline Form Sample

SUBJECT: ___Social Studies___

Topic: ___The Santa Fe Trail___

	General	**Specific**
Who:	Settlers	Mostly men, some with families
What:	Santa Fe Trail was a trade route	800 miles long
Where:	from Independence, MO. to Santa Fe, N.M.	
When:	1820's	
How:	prairie schooners (covered wagons)	
Why:	settlers used trail to move west and for trading purposes	Santa Fe didn't have adequate supplies
Vocabulary:	prairie schooners trade route	

Mapping Form Sample

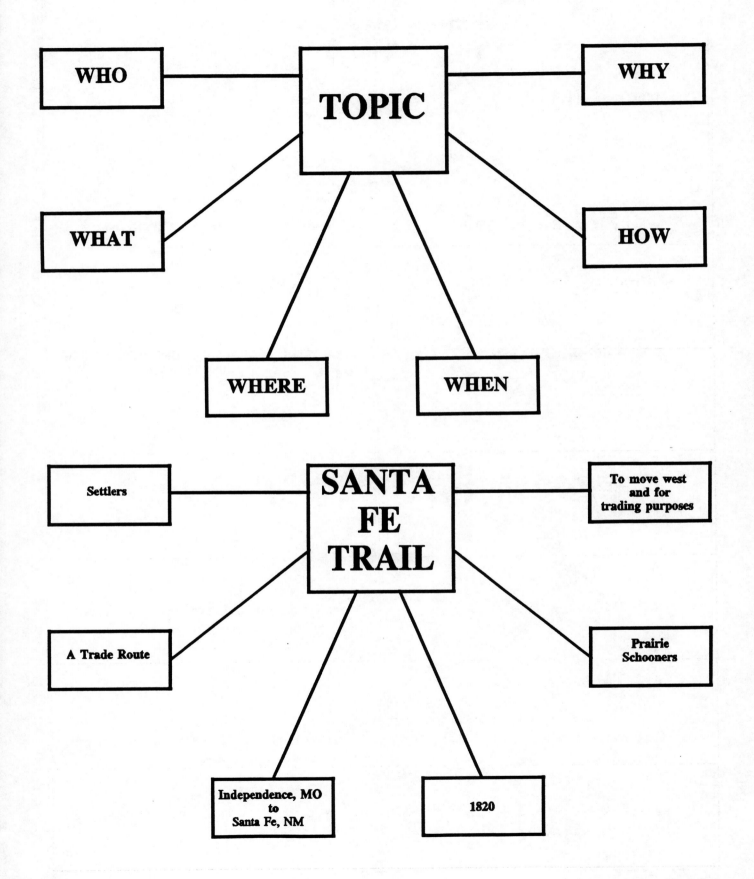

Double-Column Form Sample

SECTION 2:   The Santa Fe Trail

Who used this trail?	- settlers
What was the Santa Fe Trail?	- the Santa Fe Trail was a trade route
Where did the trail go?	- the trail went from Independence, Missouri, to Santa Fe, New Mexico
When did the trail begin?	- in the 1820's
How did settlers travel?	- traveled in prairie schooners (covered wagons)
Why was it used?	- settlers used the trail to move west and for trading purposes

Assignment Form Sample

Subject:_____

	General	Specific
What:	Depict Civil War scene and write related paragraph	Choose important part of book to depict, write supporting paragraph using 5 W's
How:	Choose scene from book	Make rough sketch, construct diorama
Materials:	Shoebox, Book	Clay, Construction Paper, Crayons, Etc.
When:	Due April 4 (2 weeks)	Do this weekend

Subject:_____

	General	Specific
What:	Field Trip	Zoo
How:	Bus	Leave at 8:45 - Return at 2:00
Materials:	Permission Slip	Extra $ for snacks Sack lunch
When:	Friday, June 1	Bring permission slip by Wednesday, May 30

Assignment Sheet Sample

ASSIGNMENT SHEET DATE ___4/14/91___

SUBJECT	ASSIGNMENT	DUE DATE	TEACHER SIGNATURE
Math	Do page 141, odd	4/15	SJ
Reading	Read pages 36 - 41	4/15	JC
Science	No homework	!	JC
Social Studies	Make diorama of chapter 3	4/20	JC
Spelling	Study words	FRI	JC
Other			

_____ Comments:

PARENT SIGNATURE

ASSIGNMENT SHEET DATE ___4/14/91___

SUBJECT	ASSIGNMENT	DUE DATE	TEACHER SIGNATURE
Math	Chapter 10 test	4/15	LM
History	Read chapter 12, questions	4/15	PW
Science	Vocabulary quiz	4/15	JB
English	Write persuasive paper	4/16	JT
Fine Arts/ Practical Arts	None		
Other	Bring P.E. clothes		

_____ Comments:

PARENT SIGNATURE

2-Week Project Outline Sample

DAY 1   **Determine exactly what the assignment is**
- Identify due date

DAY 2-4   **Project Preparation**
- **READ** Indian in the Cupboard
- **RESEARCH RELATED MATERIALS** in encyclopedia and research sources on Indian dwellings
- **GATHER NECESSARY MATERIALS**
  - Raw materials: sticks, gravel, clay, sand, bark
  - Commercial materials: glue, paint, string, masonite, dowels, plastic figures, pliers

DAY 5   **Summarize reading material answering:**
- Who, What, Where, When, How, Why

DAY 6   **Preliminary project construction**
- Make sketches, determine scale, make revisions

DAY 7-11   **Project construction**
- Lay out all materials
- Prepare materials to scale
- Build frame of longhouse using string, glue and sticks
- Cover frame with bark, affixing with glue
- Paint masonite board with diluted glue, sprinkle sand over entire board
- Construct fireplace
- Place longhouse over fireplace
- Paint plastic figures
- Affix figures to board

DAY 12   **Touch up work**
- Label, check that all items are secure, etc.

DAY 13   **Write paragraph from summary (Day 5)**

DAY 14   **Turn in!**

Test-Taking Skills

Prior to testing, the teacher should instruct the student in each of the following steps. The student then receives his/her own copy of "Test-Taking Skills." ✱

1. Survey entire test for the kinds of items that are included (e.g., true-false, multiple-choice, fill-in-the-blank, etc.).

2. Read all directions.

3. Underline or circle all key words in directions (e.g., locate, write, choose the best answer, identify the main idea, etc.).

4. Do not answer any items until the directions are thoroughly understood (i.e., ask the teacher for clarification if directions are not thoroughly understood).

5. Respond to all items for which the answer is known, skipping remaining items to answer later (some items may provide clues or reminders for items the student could not answer the first time through the test).

6. For those items which are difficult to answer, underline the key words (e.g., who, what, where, when, how, why) and then respond.

7. For those items still not understood, ask the teacher for clarification.

8. Go back and check all answers for accuracy (e.g., followed directions, proper use of math operations, no careless errors).

ADDITIONAL SUGGESTIONS

● In order for a statement to be true, all of the statement must be true (e.g., note words such as *all, never, always, etc.*).

● When matching, first answer items that are known, crossing off answers that are used, then go back to remaining items and make the best choice.

● Some items may provide clues or reminders for items the student could not answer the first time through the test.

● When writing an essay answer, construct the answer around Who, What, Where, When, How, and Why.

● On multiple-choice items, read all choices before responding. If any of the choices look new or different, they are probably not the correct answer.

● If a true-false item looks new or different, it is probably false.

✱ (See Appendix for a copy of "Test-Taking Skills.")

Studying for a Test

1. Identify the information to be covered on the test.

2. Identify and collect all necessary materials (e.g., textbook, notebook, etc.).

3. Identify major topics.

4. Under each topic identify major headings.

5. Under each heading identify Who, What, Where, When, How, and Why.

6. Write this information on the Outline Form
       or
   underline this information
       or
   highlight this information.

7. Make study aids such as flash cards. (See Appendix.)

8. Memorize information using the Outline Form and/or mnemonic devices.

ADDITIONAL SUGGESTIONS

● Study with a friend.

● Write practice questions from the Outline Form and answer the questions.

● If study questions are provided, answer all questions.

● Make certain that all information in the summary is thoroughly understood.

✱   (See Appendix for a copy of "Studying for a Test.")

Flash Card Study Aid

● The Flash Card Study Aid is a format for preparing for a test. The student is provided with a form that lists Who, What, Where, When, How, and Why for each topic studied (e.g., Pilgims). The Flash Card Study Aid is designed to be folded horizontally and used in flash card fashion when studying. One side is for questions the student writes while the reverse is for answers, also completed by the student. (See the sample of the Flash Card Study Aid on a subsequent page. A copy of the Flash Card Study Aid is included in the Appendix.)

Flash Card Study Aid Sample

Questions   Topic: __Pilgrims_____

Who: were the first settlers of North America?

What: did the first settlers do upon arrival?

Where: did the first settlers establish a colony?

When: did the first settlers come to North America?

How: did the first settlers survive?

Why: did the first settlers come to North America?

Topic: __Pilgrims_____

Who: Pilgrims

What: Built longhouses

Where: Plymouth, Mass.

When: 1620's

How: Learned from Indians

Why: Religious freedom

Schedule of Daily Events Sample

SCHEDULE OF DAILY EVENTS

NAME _____

	#1	#2	#3	#4	#5	#6	#7	#8	#9	#10
Monday	Reading	Art (Clay)	Math	Art (Paint)	Science	Creative Writing	Social Studies	Listening	Music	P.E.
Tuesday										
Wednesday										
Thursday										
Friday										

III. Interventions

1 Has difficulty following oral instructions

1. Provide clearly stated oral instructions (e.g., make the instructions as simple and concrete as possible).

2. Make certain that oral instructions are given at the level at which the student can be successful (e.g., two-step or three-step directions are not given to students who can only successfully follow one-step directions).

3. Present instructions in both written and verbal form.

4. Provide the student with a written copy of oral instructions.

5. Tape record instructions for the student to listen to individually and repeat as necessary.

6. Maintain consistency in the format of oral instructions.

7. Speak to the student to explain: (a) what he/she is doing wrong (e.g., ignoring oral instructions), and (b) what he/she should be doing (e.g., listening to and following oral instructions).

8. Reinforce the student for following oral instructions based on the length of time he/she can be successful. Gradually increase the length of time required for reinforcement as the student demonstrates success.

9. Reduce distracting stimuli in order to increase the student's ability to follow oral instructions (e.g., place the student on the front row, provide a carrel or "office space" away from distractions, etc.). This is used as a means of reducing distracting stimuli and not as a form of punishment.

10. Structure the environment in such a way as to provide the student with increased opportunity for help or assistance on academic tasks (e.g., peer tutoring, directions for work sent home, frequent interactions, etc.).

11. Write a contract with the student specifying what behavior is expected (e.g., following oral instructions) and what reinforcement will be made available when the terms of the contract have been met.

12. Evaluate the appropriateness of the task to determine: (a) if the task is too difficult, and (b) if the length of time scheduled to complete the task is appropriate.

13. Identify a peer to act as a model for the student to imitate following oral instructions.

14. Have the student question any oral directions, explanations, instructions he/she does not understand.

15. Assign a peer to work with the student to help him/her follow oral directions.

16. Teach the student verbal direction-following skills (e.g., listen carefully, write down important points, use environmental cues, wait until all directions are received before beginning, etc.).

17. Give directions in a variety of ways in order to increase the probability of understanding (e.g., if the student fails to understand oral instructions, present them in written form).

18. Interact frequently with the student in order to help him/her follow oral instructions for the activity.

19. Work the first problem or problems with the student in order to make certain that he/she follows the oral instructions accurately.

20. Provide alternatives for the traditional format of presenting oral instructions (e.g., tape record, summarize instructions, instructions given by peers, etc.).

21. Have the student practice verbal direction-following on nonacademic tasks (e.g., recipes, games, etc.).

22. Have the student repeat instructions or give an interpretation after receiving oral instructions.

23. Reduce verbal to steps (e.g., give the student each additional step after completion of the previous step).

24. Deliver a predetermined signal (e.g., clapping hands, turning lights off and on, etc.) before giving oral instructions.

25. Give oral instructions before handing out materials.

26. Make certain the student achieves success when following oral instructions.

27. Reduce emphasis on competition. Competitive activities may cause the student to hurry to begin the task without following oral instructions.

28. Communicate clearly to the student when it is time to listen to oral instructions.

29. Develop instruction-following assignments/activities (e.g., informal activities designed to have the student carry out oral instructions in steps, with increasing degrees of difficulty).

30. Require the student to wait until the teacher gives him/her a signal before beginning the task (e.g., give a hand signal, ring a bell, etc.).

31. Make certain the student is attending to the teacher (e.g., making eye contact, hands free of writing materials, looking at assignment, etc.) before giving oral instructions.

32. Stand next to the student when giving oral instructions.

33. Have a designated person be the only individual to deliver oral instructions to the student.

34. Maintain visibility to and from the student. The teacher should be able to see the student and the student should be able to see the teacher, making eye contact possible at all times when giving oral instructions.

35. Make certain that oral instructions are delivered in a supportive rather than in a threatening manner (e.g., "Will you please. . ." or "You need . . ." rather than "You better . . ." or "If you don't . . .").

36. Make certain the student has all the materials needed to perform the assignment/activity.

37. Have a peer help the student with any oral instructions he/she does not understand.

38. Seat the student close to the source of the oral instructions (e.g., teacher, aide, peer, etc.).

39. Seat the student far enough away from peers in order to ensure increased opportunities for attending to oral instructions.

40. Work through the steps of the oral instructions as they are delivered in order to make certain the student follows the instructions accurately (i.e., have the student follow the steps of the instructions as they are given).

41. Have the student carry out one step of the oral instructions at a time, checking with the teacher to make certain that each step is successfully followed before attempting the next.

42. Present instructions following the outline of: (1) What, (2) How, (3) Materials, and (4) When.

43. Have the student take notes when instructions are being given following the "What, How, Materials, and When" format. (See Appendix for Assignment Form.)

44. Have the student listen and take notes for "Who, What, Where, When, How, and Why" while concepts are presented. (See Appendix for Outline Form.)

45. Present concepts following the outline of: (1) Who, (2) What, (3) Where, (4) When, (5) How, and (6) Why.

46. Have the student prepare for tests using the "Who, What, Where, When, How, and Why" system. (See Appendix for Outline Form.)

2 Does not hear all of what is said

1. Make certain the student's hearing has been checked recently.

2. Identify a list of key words that the student will practice listening for when someone is speaking.

3. Speak to the student to explain: (a) what he/she is doing wrong (e.g., failing to listen for key words) and (b) what he/she should be doing (e.g., listening for key words).

4. Evaluate the level of difficulty of information to which the student is expected to listen (e.g., information should be communicated on the student's ability level).

5. Have the student question any directions, explanations, instructions he/she does not understand.

6. Have the student repeat or paraphrase what is said to him/her in order to determine what was heard.

7. Give the student short directions, explanations, and instructions to follow. Gradually increase the length of the directions, explanations, and instructions as the student demonstrates success.

8. Maintain consistency in the verbal delivery of information.

9. Make certain the student is attending to the source of information (e.g., making eye contact, hands free of writing materials, looking at assignment, etc.).

10. Provide the student with written directions and instructions to supplement verbal directions and instructions.

11. Emphasize or repeat key words, due dates, quantity, etc.

12. Speak clearly and concisely when delivering directions, explanations, and instructions.

13. Place the student near the source of information.

14. Reduce distracting stimuli (e.g., noise and motion in the classroom) in order to enhance the student's ability to listen successfully.

15. Stop at key points when delivering directions, explanations, and instructions in order to determine student comprehension.

16. Deliver directions, explanations, and instructions at an appropriate pace.

17. Present directions following the outline of: (1) What, (2) How, (3) Materials, and (4) When.

18. Have the student take notes when directions are being given following the "What, How, Materials, and When" format. (See Appendix for Assignment Form.)

19. Have the student listen and take notes for "Who, What, Where, When, How, and Why" while concepts are presented. (See Appendix for Outline Form.)

20. Present concepts following the outline of: (1) Who, (2) What, (3) Where, (4) When, (5) How, and (6) Why.

21. Have the student prepare for tests using the "Who, What, Where, When, How, and Why" system. (See Appendix for Outline Form.)

3 Does not direct attention or fails to maintain attention

1. Make certain the student's hearing has been checked recently.

2. Reinforce the student for directing and maintaining his/her attention to important sounds in the immediate environment based on the length of time the student can be successful. Gradually increase the length of time required for reinforcement as the student demonstrates success.

3. Identify a peer to act as a model for the student to imitate directing and maintaining his/her attention to important sounds in the immediate environment.

4. Have the student question any directions/ explanations he/she does not understand.

5. Seat the student close to the source of sound.

6. Make certain the student is attending (e.g., making eye contact, hands free of materials, etc.) before delivering directions, explanations, instructions.

7. Make certain that competing sounds (e.g., talking, movement, noises, etc.) are silenced when directions are being given, public address announcements are being made, etc.

8. Deliver a predetermined signal (e.g., hand signal, turning lights off and on, etc.) prior to bells ringing, announcements being made, directions being given, etc.

9. Give a verbal cue in order to gain the student's attention prior to bells ringing, announcements being made, etc.

10. Stand directly in front of the student when delivering information.

11. Call the student by name prior to bells ringing, announcements being made, directions being delivered, etc.

12. Seat the student next to a peer who directs and maintains his/her attention to important sounds in the immediate environment.

13. Have a peer provide the student with the information he/she does not hear.

14. Provide the student with public announcements, directions, and instructions in written form.

15. Maintain visibility to and from the student at all times in order to ensure that he/she is attending.

16. Reduce distracting stimuli in the immediate environment (e.g., place the student on the front row, provide the student with a carrel or "office" space away from distractions, etc.). This is used as a means of reducing distracting stimuli and not as a form of punishment.

17. Have the student verbally repeat information he/she hears.

18. Teach the student listening skills (e.g., listen carefully, write down important points, ask for clarification, wait until all directions are received before beginning, etc.).

19. Have the student engage in practice activities designed to develop his/her listening skills (e.g., following one-, two-, and three-step directions; listening for the main point, etc.).

20. Make certain that directions, public announcements, etc., are delivered in a clear and concise manner (e.g., keep phrases and sentences short).

21. Give directions in a variety of ways in order to enhance the student's ability to attend.

22. Stop at various points when delivering directions, public announcements, etc., in order to ensure that the student is attending.

23. Deliver directions one step at a time. Gradually increase the number of steps as the student demonstrates the ability to direct and maintain his/her attention.

24. Maintain consistency of the format in which auditory information in the immediate environment is delivered (e.g., morning announcements, recess bells, delivering directions, etc.).

25. Seat the student far enough from peers in order to ensure his/her ability to successfully attend to important sounds in the immediate environment.

26. Have the student listen and take notes for "Who, What, Where, When, How, and Why" while concepts are presented. (See Appendix for Outline Form.)

27. Present concepts following the outline of: (1) Who, (2) What, (3) Where, (4) When, (5) How, and (6) Why.

28. Have the student prepare for tests using the "Who, What, Where, When, How, and Why" system. (See Appendix for Outline Form.)

29. Present directions following the outline of: (1) What, (2) How, (3) Materials, and (4) When.

30. Have the student take notes when directions are being given following the "What, How, Materials, and When" format. (See Appendix for Assignment Form.)

1. Make certain the student's hearing has been checked recently.

2. Speak to the student to explain: (a) what he/she is doing wrong (e.g., not listening to directions, explanations, and instructions), and (b) what he/she should be doing (e.g., listening to directions, explanations, and instructions).

3. Evaluate the level of difficulty of information to which the student is expected to listen (e.g., information communicated on the student's ability level).

4. Identify a peer to act as a model for the student to imitate appropriate listening skills.

5. Have the student question any directions, explanations, instructions, he/she does not understand.

6. Seat the student close to the source of directions, explanations, and instructions.

7. Make certain the student is attending (e.g., making eye contact, hands free of writing materials, etc.) before delivering directions, explanations, and instructions.

8. Make certain that competing sounds (e.g., talking, movement, noises, etc.) are silenced when directions are being given, public address announcements are being made, etc.

9. Deliver a predetermined signal (e.g., hand signal, turning lights off and on, etc.) prior to bells ringing, announcements being made, etc.

10. Stand directly in front of the student when delivering directions, explanations, and instructions.

11. Call the student by name prior to bells ringing, announcements being made, directions being given, etc.

12. Provide the student with public announcements, directions, and instructions in written form.

13. Have a peer provide the student with the information he/she does not hear.

14. Maintain visibility to and from the student at all times to ensure that he/she is attending.

15. Reduce distracting stimuli in the immediate environment (e.g., place the student on the front row, provide the student with a carrel or "office" space away from distractions, etc.). This is used as a means of reducing distracting stimuli and not as a form of punishment.

16. Have the student verbally repeat or paraphrase information he/she hears.

17. Teach the student listening skills (e.g., listen carefully, write down important points, ask for clarification, wait until all directions are received before beginning).

18. Have the student engage in practice activities designed to develop his/her listening skills (e.g., following one-, two-, and three-step directions; listening for the main point, etc.).

19. Give directions in a variety of ways in order to enhance the student's ability to attend.

20. Stop at various points when delivering directions, public announcements, etc., in order to ensure that the student is attending.

21. Deliver directions to the student individually.

22. Demonstrate directions, explanations, and instructions as they are presented orally (e.g., use the chalkboard to work a problem for the student, begin playing a game with the student, etc.).

23. Use pictures, diagrams, and gestures when delivering information.

24. Deliver information slowly to the student.

25. Present one concept at a time. Make certain the student understands each concept before presenting the next.

26. Rephrase directions, explanations, and instructions in order to increase the likelihood of the student understanding what is being presented.

27. Present directions, explanations, and instructions as simply and clearly as possible (e.g., "Get your book. Turn to page 29. Do problems 1-5.").

28. When delivering directions, explanations, and instructions, be certain to use vocabulary that is within the student's level of comprehension.

29. Have the student practice listening skills by taking notes when directions, explanations, or announcements are presented. (See Appendix for Assignment Form.)

30. Play games designed to teach listening skills (e.g., "Simon Says," "Red Light, Green Light," "Mother May I," etc.).

31. Have the student practice group listening skills (e.g., "Everyone take out a piece of paper. Write your name on the paper. Number your paper from 1 to 20.").

32. Teach the student when to ask questions, how to ask questions, and what types of questions obtain what types of information.

33. Have the student repeat to himself/herself information just heard in order to help him/her remember the important facts.

34. Have the student use listening or study guides supplied by the teacher.

35. Present directions following the outline of: (1) What, (2) How, (3) Materials, and (4) When.

36. Have the student take notes when directions are being given following the "What, How, Materials, and When" format. (See Appendix for Assignment Form.)

37. Have the student listen and take notes for the "Who, What, Where, When, How, and Why" while concepts are presented. (See Appendix for Outline Form.)

38. Present concepts following the outline of: (1) Who, (2) What, (3) Where, (4) When, (5) How, and (6) Why.

39. Have the student prepare for tests using the "Who, What, Where, When, How, and Why" system. (See Appendix for Outline Form.)

5 Requires a one-to-one situation in order to follow directions

1. Make certain the student's hearing has been checked recently.

2. Speak to the student to explain: (a) what he/she is doing wrong (e.g., failing to follow directions, explanations, and instructions), and (b) what he/she should be doing (e.g., following directions, explanations, and instructions).

3. Reinforce those students in the classroom who follow directions, explanations, and instructions.

4. Reinforce the student for listening based on the length of time the student can be successful. Gradually increase the length of time required for reinforcement as the student demonstrates success.

5. Write a contract with the student specifying what behavior is expected (e.g., following directions, explanations, and instructions) and what reinforcement will be made available when the terms of the contract have been met.

6. Have the student question any directions, explanations, instructions he/she does not understand.

7. Determine which stimuli in the environment interfere with the student's ability to listen successfully. Reduce or remove those stimuli from the environment.

8. Remove the distracting stimuli in the student's immediate environment (e.g., books, writing materials, personal property, etc.).

9. Reduce visual and auditory stimuli in and around the classroom which interfere with the student's ability to listen successfully and follow directions (e.g., close the classroom door and windows, draw the shades, etc.).

10. Make certain information is delivered loudly enough to be heard by the student.

11. Deliver information to the student on a one-to-one basis. Gradually include more students in the group with the student as he/she demonstrates the ability to listen successfully.

12. Maintain eye contact when delivering information to the student. Gradually decrease the amount of eye contact as the student demonstrates the ability to listen successfully.

13. Deliver information in a clear and concise manner.

14. Deliver information in both verbal and written form.

15. Evaluate the level of information presented to the student to determine if the information is presented at a level the student can understand.

16. Maintain visibility to and from the student at all times in order to ensure that he/she is attending.

17. Seat the student close to the source of information in the classroom. Gradually move the student farther away from the source of information as he/she demonstrates success.

18. Make certain the student is not engaged in activities that interfere with directions, explanations, and instructions (e.g., looking at other materials, putting away materials, talking to others, etc.).

19. Require the student to repeat or paraphrase information heard in order to determine successful listening.

20. Teach the student listening skills (e.g., have hands free of writing materials, clear desk of nonessential materials, attend to the source of information, etc.) in order to enhance his/her ability to listen successfully.

21. Deliver a predetermined signal to the student (e.g., hand signal, turn lights off and on, etc.) prior to delivering information.

22. Verbally present information that is necessary for the student to have in order to be able to perform successfully.

23. Have the student take notes when information is verbally presented.

24. Maintain consistency in the format in which information is verbally presented.

25. Call the student by name prior to delivering information.

26. Make certain that the student is seated close enough to see and hear the teacher when information is being delivered.

27. Present directions following the outline of: (1) What, (2) How, (3) Materials, and (4) When.

28. Have the student take notes when directions are being given following the "What, How, Materials, and When" format. (See Appendix for Assignment Form.)

6 Has difficulty with short-term or long-term memory

1. Make certain the student's hearing has been checked recently.

2. Write a contract with the student specifying what behavior is expected (e.g., following one-step directions, two-step directions, etc.) and what reinforcement will be made available when the terms of the contract have been met.

3. Evaluate the appropriateness of the memory activities to determine: (a) if the task is too difficult, and (b) if the length of time scheduled to complete the task is appropriate.

4. Have the student question any directions, explanations, instructions he/she does not understand.

5. Have the student act as a classroom messenger. Give the student a verbal message to deliver to another teacher, secretary, administrator, etc. Increase the length of the messages as the student demonstrates success.

6. Review the schedule of morning or afternoon activities with the student and have him/her repeat the sequence. Increase the length of the sequence as the student is successful.

7. Have the student engage in concentration game activities with a limited number of symbols. Gradually increase the number of symbols as the student demonstrates success.

8. Reinforce students for remembering to have such materials as pens, pencils, paper, textbooks, notebooks, etc.

9. At the end of the school day, have the student recall three activities in which he/she was engaged during the day. Gradually increase the number of activities the student is required to recall as he/she demonstrates success.

10. Record a message on tape. Have the student write the message after he/she has heard it. Increase the length of the message as the student demonstrates success.

11. After a field trip or special event, have the student sequence the activities which occurred.

12. After reading a short story, have the student identify the main characters, sequence the events, and report the outcome of the story.

13. Have the student tell the schedule of daily events to other students.

14. Use multiple modalities (e.g., auditory, visual, tactile, etc.) when presenting directions, explanations, and instructional content.

15. Assign a peer tutor to engage in short-term memory activities with the student (e.g., concentration games, following directions, etc.).

16. Involve the student in activities in order to enhance his/her short-term memory skills (e.g., carry messages from one location to another, act as group leader or teacher assistant, etc.).

17. Have the student practice short-term memory skills by engaging in activities which are purposeful to him/her (e.g., delivering messages, being in charge of room clean-up, acting as custodian's helper, operating equipment, etc.).

18. Informally assess the student's auditory and visual short-term memory skills in order to determine which is the stronger. Utilize the results when presenting directions, explanations, and instructional content.

19. Have the student practice repetition of information in order to increase short-term memory skills (e.g., repeating names, telephone numbers, dates of events, etc.).

20. Teach the student how to organize information into smaller units (e.g., break the number sequence 132563 into units of 13, 25, 63).

21. Show the student an object or a picture of an object for a few seconds. Ask the student to recall specific attributes of the object (e.g., color, size, shape, etc.).

22. Use sentence dictation to develop the student's short-term memory skills (e.g., begin with sentences of three words and increase the length of the sentences as the student demonstrates success).

23. Deliver directions, explanations, and instructional content in a clear manner and at an appropriate pace.

24. Have the student practice making notes for specific information he/she wants and/or needs to remember.

25. Teach the student to recognize key words and phrases related to information in order to increase his/her short-term or long-term memory skills.

26. Make certain the student is attending (e.g., eye contact is being made, hands are free of materials, student is looking at assignment, etc.) to the source of information.

27. Reduce distracting stimuli when information is being presented or when the student is studying, etc.

28. Stop at various points during the presentation of information to check the student's comprehension.

29. Give the student one task to perform at a time. Introduce the next task only when the student has successfully completed the previous task.

30. Have the student memorize the first sentence or line of poems, songs, etc. Require more to be memorized as the student experiences success.

31. Have the student repeat/paraphrase directions, explanations, and instructions.

32. Teach the student information-gathering skills (e.g., listen carefully, write down important points, ask for clarification, wait until all information is received before beginning, etc.).

33. Reduce the emphasis on competition. Competitive activities may increase the student's anxiety and may cause the student to not remember information.

34. Provide the student with environmental cues and prompts designed to increase short-term or long-term memory (e.g., posted rules, Schedule of Daily Events, steps for performing tasks, etc.). (See Appendix for Schedule of Daily Events.)

35. Provide the student with written lists of things to do, materials he/she will need, etc.

36. Establish a regular routine for the student to follow in performing activities, assignments, etc. (e.g., listen to the person speaking to you, wait until directions are completed, make certain you have all necessary materials, etc.).

37. Maintain consistency in sequential activities in order to increase the likelihood of student success (e.g., the student has math every day at one o'clock, recess at two o'clock, etc.).

38. Teach the student to use associative cues or mnemonic devices to remember sequences.

39. Actively involve the student in learning to remember sequences by having the student physically perform sequential activities (e.g., operating equipment, following recipes, solving math problems, etc.).

40. Have the student be responsible for helping a peer remember sequences.

41. Use concrete examples and experiences in sharing information with the student.

42. Teach the student to rely on resources in the environment to recall information (e.g., notes, textbooks, pictures, etc.).

43. When the student is required to recall information, provide him/her with auditory cues to help him/her remember the information (e.g., key words, a brief oral description to clue the student, etc.).

44. Teach the student to recognize main points, important facts, etc.

45. Assess the meaningfulness of the material to the student. Remembering is more likely to occur when the student can relate to real experiences.

46. Relate the information being presented to the student's previous experiences.

47. Help the student employ memory aids in order to recall words (e.g., a name might be linked to another word; for example, "Mr. Green is a very colorful person.").

48. Have the student outline, highlight, underline, or summarize information he/she should remember.

49. Make certain the student has adequate opportunities for repetition of information through different experiences in order to enhance his/her memory.

50. Present directions following the outline of: (1) What, (2) How, (3) Materials, and (4) When.

51. Label objects, persons, places, etc., in the environment in order to help the student be able to recall their names.

52. Make certain the student receives information from a variety of sources (e.g., texts, discussions, films, slide presentations, etc.) in order to enhance the student's memory/recall.

53. Have the student take notes when directions are being given following the "What, How, Materials, and When" format. (See Appendix for Assignment Form.)

54. Have the student listen and take notes for "Who, What, Where, When, How, and Why" while concepts are presented. (See Appendix for Outline Form.)

55. Present concepts following the outline of: (1) Who, (2) What, (3) Where, (4) When, (5) How, and (6) Why.

56. Have the student prepare for tests using the "Who, What, Where, When, How, and Why" system. (See Appendix for Outline Form.)

7 Does not respond appropriately to environmental cues

1. Speak to the student to explain: (a) what he/she is doing wrong (e.g., failing to respond appropriately to bells, signs indicating rest room directions, etc.), and (b) what he/she should be doing (e.g., responding appropriately to bells, signs indicating rest room directions, etc.).

2. Reinforce the student for responding appropriately to environmental cues based on the number of environmental cues the student can successfully follow. Gradually increase the number of environmental cues required for reinforcement as the student demonstrates success.

3. Write a contract with the student specifying what behavior is expected (e.g., responding appropriately to bells, rules, point cards, reminders, etc.) and what reinforcement will be made available when the terms of the contract have been met.

4. Evaluate the appropriateness of the environmental cues the student is expected to follow in order to determine: (a) if the cue is too difficult, and (b) if the length of time required to respond to the cue is appropriate.

5. Identify a peer to act as a model for the student to imitate appropriate responses to environmental cues.

6. Have the student question any environmental cues he/she does not understand.

7. Establish environmental cues that the student is expected to follow (e.g., bells, rules, point cards, reminders, etc.).

8. Provide supportive information to assist the student in responding appropriately to environmental cues (e.g., match bells ringing to the time of the day in order that the student will know that he/she should go to another class, lunch, leave the building, etc.).

9. Provide repeated practice in responding appropriately to environmental cues.

10. Make the student responsible for identifying environmental cues for his/her peers (e.g., bells, rules, reminders, etc.).

11. Provide the student with universal environmental cues (e.g., symbols for male and female, arrows, exit signs, danger symbols, etc.).

12. Pair environmental cues with verbal explanations and provide immediate reinforcement for appropriately responding.

13. Prepare the student in advance of the delivery of environmental cues in order to increase successful responding.

14. Make certain the same environmental cues are used throughout all locations in and outside the building.

15. Match environmental cues to the student's ability to respond (e.g., visual cues are used for students who cannot hear, symbols or auditory cues are used for students who cannot read, etc.).

16. Model appropriate responses to environmental cues for the student to imitate.

17. Have the student master appropriate responding to one environmental cue at a time, prioritizing environmental cues in order of importance for mastery before introducing additional cues.

18. In order to increase success in learning environmental cues, have the student observe and imitate the responses of his/her peers to environmental cues (e.g., as the student is learning to respond appropriately to doors identified as "In" and "Out," he/she can imitate the behavior of peers who use the appropriate doors to enter and leave an area of the educational environment).

19. Reinforce the student for asking the meaning of environmental cues he/she does not understand (e.g., bells, signs, etc.).

20. Provide the student with stimulating activities in the classroom in order to teach him/her successful responses to environmental cues (e.g., responses to words, symbols, directions, etc.).

21. Assign a peer to accompany the student as he/she moves throughout the educational environment to act as a tutor in teaching appropriate responses to environmental cues.

8 Needs oral questions and directions frequently repeated

1. Make certain the student's hearing has been checked recently.

2. Speak with the student to explain: (a) what he/she is doing wrong (e.g., needing oral questions and directions repeated), and (b) what he/she should be doing (e.g., responding to oral questions and directions without requiring repetition).

3. Establish classroom rules (e.g., work on task, work quietly, remain in your seat, finish task, meet task expectations). Reiterate rules often and reinforce students for following rules.

4. Reinforce the student for responding to oral questions and directions without requiring repetition based on the number of times he/she can be successful. Gradually increase the number of times required for reinforcement as the student demonstrates success.

5. Write a contract with the student specifying what behavior is expected (e.g, following directions with one cue) and what reinforcement will be made available when the terms of the contract have been met.

6. Identify a peer to act as a model for the student to imitate responding to oral questions and directions without requiring repetition.

7. Have the student question any directions, explanations, instructions he/she does not understand.

8. Evaluate the appropriateness of requiring the student to respond to oral questions and directions without needing repetition.

9. Present oral questions and directions in a clear and concise manner.

10. Have the student take notes relative to oral directions.

11. Reduce distracting stimuli (e.g., place the student on the front row, provide a carrel or "office" space away from distractions, etc.). This is used as a means of reducing distracting stimuli and not as a form of punishment.

12. Have a peer help the student follow oral directions.

13. Maintain mobility in order to provide assistance to the student.

14. Present oral questions and directions in a variety of ways in order to increase the probability of understanding (e.g., if the student fails to understand verbal directions, present them in written form).

15. Maintain consistency in the manner in which oral questions and directions are delivered.

16. Deliver oral questions and directions that involve only one concept or step. Gradually increase the number of concepts or steps as the student demonstrates success.

17. Stand close to or directly in front of the student when delivering oral questions and directions.

18. Teach the student listening skills (e.g., stop working, look at the person delivering questions and directions, have necessary note-taking materials, etc.).

19. Deliver questions and directions in written form.

20. Identify a peer to deliver and/or repeat oral questions and directions.

21. Give a signal prior to delivering directions orally to the student.

22. Deliver oral directions prior to handing out materials.

23. Teach the student direction-following skills (e.g., listen carefully, write down important points, etc.).

24. Gradually increase expectations that the student will be given directions only once. Make certain that the student understands that the goal is to follow directions after directions are given the first time.

25. Interact frequently with the student in order to help him/her follow directions.

26. Have the student repeat or paraphrase the directions orally to the teacher.

27. Establish assignment rules (e.g., listen to directions, wait until all oral directions have been given, ask questions about anything you do not understand, begin the assignment only when you are certain about what you are supposed to do, make certain you have all necessary materials, etc.).

28. Make certain the student is attending while you deliver oral questions and directions (e.g., making eye contact, hands free of writing materials, looking at assignment, etc.).

29. Maintain visibility to and from the student when delivering oral questions and directions. The teacher should be able to see the student and the student should be able to see the teacher, making eye contact possible at all times in order to make certain the student is attending.

30. Call the student by name prior to delivering oral questions and directions.

31. Present directions following the outline of: (1) What, (2) How, (3) Materials, and (4) When.

32. Have the student take notes when directions are being given following the "What, How, Materials, and When" format. (See Appendix for Assignment Form.)

1. Make certain the student's hearing has been checked recently.

2. Draw the student's attention to key aspects of auditory communications as they occur (e.g., repeat important points, call the student by name, tell the student which information is particularly important, etc.).

3. Evaluate the appropriateness of the task to determine: (a) if the task is too difficult (e.g., too much information to remember), or (b) if the length of time required for the student to remember is inappropriate (e.g., presentation of information was too brief or time lapse between presentation of material and request for recall was too long).

4. Provide the student with more than one source of directions, explanations, instructions, etc., before requiring him/her to remember.

5. When the student is required to recall information, provide him/her with auditory cues to help him/her remember the information previously presented (e.g., say, "Remember yesterday when I said . . ." etc.).

6. Provide visual information to support information the student receives auditorily.

7. Teach the student to learn sequences and lists of information in segments (e.g., telephone numbers are learned as 874, then 1710).

8. Gradually have the student follow verbal one-, two-, and three-step directions.

9. Provide the student with verbal directions, rules, lists, etc. Reinforce the student for being able to recall information which is presented in verbal form.

10. Write stories, directions, etc., so the student may listen as he/she reads along.

11. Tell the student what to listen for before delivering auditory information.

12. Send the student on errands to deliver verbal messages to other teachers in the building.

13. Be certain that auditory information is presented slowly enough for the student to know what is being presented.

14. While reading a story to the student, stop on occasion to ask questions about the plot, main characters, events in the story, etc.

15. Have the student pretend he/she is a waiter/waitress. Have the student recall as much as possible from an order given to him/her.

16. Have the student paraphrase directions, explanations, and instructions soon after hearing them.

17. Use as much visual information as possible when teaching (e.g., chalkboard, overhead projections, pictures, etc.).

18. Have the student tape record directions, explanations, and instructions in order to be able to replay needed information.

19. Use simple, concise sentences to convey information to the student.

20. Have the student recall names of friends, days of the week, months of the year, addresses, telephone numbers, etc.

21. After listening to a tape, story, record, etc., have the student recall characters, main events, sequence of events, etc.

22. Have the student read along while listening to a taped story or book.

23. Present directions following the outline of: (1) What, (2) How, (3) Materials, and (4) When.

24. Have the student take notes when directions are being given following the "What, How, Materials, and When" format. (See Appendix for Assignment Form.)

25. Have the student listen and take notes for "Who, What, Where, When, How, and Why" while concepts are presented. (See Appendix for Outline Form.)

26. Present concepts following the outline of: (1) Who, (2) What, (3) Where, (4) When, (5) How, and (6) Why.

27. Have the student prepare for tests using the "Who, What, Where, When, How, and Why" system. (See Appendix for Outline Form.)

10 Has difficulty attending when directions are given

1. Establish classroom rules (e.g., work on task, work quietly, remain in your seat, finish task, meet task expectations, etc.). Reiterate rules often and reinforce students for following rules.

2. Reinforce the student for attending to a task for the length of time the student can be successful. Gradually increase the length of time required for reinforcement.

3. Write a contract with the student specifying what behavior is expected (e.g., attending to a task) and what reinforcement will be made available when the terms of the contract have been met.

4. Assess the quality and clarity of directions, explanations, and instructions given to the student.

5. Structure the environment in such a way as to reduce distracting stimuli (e.g., place the student on the front row, provide a carrel or quiet place away from distractions, etc.). This is used as a means of reducing distracting stimuli and not as a form of punishment.

6. Follow a less desirable task with a more desirable task, making the completion of the first necessary to perform the second.

7. Break down large tasks into smaller tasks (e.g., assign the student to write an outline for a book report, then the first rough draft, etc.).

8. Assign a peer tutor to work directly with the student to serve as a model for appropriate work habits.

9. Give directions in a variety of ways to increase the probability of understanding (e.g., if the student fails to understand verbal directions, present them in written form).

10. Provide clearly stated directions, written or verbal (e.g., make directions as simple and concrete as possible).

11. Make certain the student knows that directions will only be given once.

12. Reduce directions to steps (e.g., give the student each additional step after completion of the previous step).

13. Try various groupings in order to determine the situation in which the student attends most easily.

14. Separate the student from peers who may be encouraging or stimulating the inappropriate behavior.

15. Reinforce the student for beginning, staying on, and completing assignments.

16. Assign the student shorter tasks and gradually increase the number over time as the student demonstrates success.

17. Use a variety of high-interest means to communicate with the student (e.g., auditory, visual, manipulatives, etc.).

18. Present assignments in small amounts (e.g., assign 10 problems, use pages removed from workbooks, etc.).

19. Make certain that the student's academic tasks are on his/her ability level.

20. Maintain physical contact with the student while talking to him/her (e.g., touch the student's hand or shoulder).

21. Require the student to make eye contact while delivering information to him/her.

22. Deliver one-, two-, and three-step directions to the student, increasing the number of steps as the student demonstrates success in concentrating.

23. Have the student participate in games which require varying times of attending (e.g., tic-tac-toe, checkers, chess, etc.).

24. Reduce distracting stimuli in and around the student's desk (e.g., materials in the desk, on the desk, etc.).

25. Seat the student close to the source of information.

26. Highlight or underline important information the student reads (e.g., directions, reading assignments, math word problems, etc.).

27. Tell the student what to listen for when being given directions, receiving information, etc.

11 Does not follow directives from teachers or other school personnel

1. Speak with the student to explain: (a) what he/she is doing wrong (e.g., failing to follow directions or observe rules), and (b) what he/she should be doing (e.g., following established guidelines or expectations).

2. Establish classroom rules (e.g., work on task, work quietly, remain in your seat, finish task, meet task expectations). Reiterate rules often and reinforce students for following rules.

3. Reinforce the student for following the directives of teachers and other school personnel based on the length of time he/she can be successful. Gradually increase the amount of time required for reinforcement as the student demonstrates success.

4. Write a contract with the student specifying what behavior is expected (e.g., following teacher directives) and what reinforcement will be made available when the terms of the contract have been met.

5. Evaluate the appropriateness of the task to determine: (a) if the task is too difficult, and (b) if the length of time scheduled for the task is appropriate.

6. Structure the environment in such a way that the student remains active and involved in appropriate behavior.

7. Maintain visibility to and from the student. The teacher should be able to see the student and the student should be able to see the teacher, making eye contact possible at all times.

8. Maintain maximum supervision of the student and gradually decrease supervision as the student becomes successful at following directives.

9. Be mobile in order to be frequently near the student.

10. Provide the student with many social and academic successes.

11. Provide the student with positive feedback which indicates he/she is successful.

12. Post rules in various places, including on the student's desk.

13. Make certain the student receives the information necessary to perform activities (e.g., written information, verbal directions, reminders).

14. Teach the student direction-following skills: (a) listen carefully, (b) ask questions, (c) use environmental cues, (d) rely on examples provided, (e) wait until all directions are given before beginning, etc.

15. Maintain a positive, professional relationship with the student (e.g., an adversary relationship is likely to result in failure to follow directions).

16. Be a consistent authority figure (e.g., be consistent in relationship with the student).

17. Provide the student with optional courses of action in order to prevent total refusal to obey directives from teachers and other school personnel.

18. Deliver directions in a step-by-step sequence.

19. Have a peer act as a model for following teacher directives.

20. Interact with the student frequently to determine if directives are being followed.

21. Maintain consistency in rules, routine, and general expectations of conduct and procedure.

22. Limit the student's opportunity to engage in activities in which he/she does not follow directives from teachers and other school personnel (e.g., recess, industrial arts activities, field trips, etc.).

23. Present directions following the outline of: (1) What, (2) How, (3) Materials, and (4) When.

24. Have the student take notes when directions are being given following the "What, How, Materials, and When" format. (See Appendix for Assignment Form.)

12 Begins assignments before receiving directions or instructions, or does not follow directions or instructions

1. Speak with the student to explain: (a) what he/she is doing wrong (e.g., not following directions when performing academic tasks), and (b) what he/she should be doing (e.g., listening to directions, asking for clarification if directions are not understood, taking notes, following one step at a time, etc.).

2. Establish classroom rules (e.g., work on task, work quietly, remain in your seat, finish task, meet task expectations). Reiterate rules often and reinforce students for following rules.

3. Reinforce the student for beginning assignments after receiving directions, instructions, etc., based on the length of time the student can be successful. Gradually decrease the amount of time to begin the task in order for the student to be reinforced.

4. Write a contract with the student specifying what behavior is expected (e.g., beginning assignments after listening to directions) and what reinforcement will be made available when the terms of the contract have been met.

5. Evaluate the appropriateness of assigned tasks to determine: (a) if the task is too difficult, and (b) if the length of time scheduled is appropriate.

6. Have the student question any directions, explanations, and instructions he/she does not understand.

7. Assess the quality and clarity of directions, explanations, and instructions given to the student.

8. Assign a peer or volunteer to help the student begin a task.

9. Structure the environment in such a way as to provide the student with increased opportunities for help or assistance.

10. Reduce distracting stimuli (e.g., place the student in the front row, provide a carrel or "office" space away from distractions, etc.). This is used as a means of reducing distracting stimuli and not as a form of punishment.

11. Communicate clearly to the student when it is time to begin.

12. Maintain mobility in order to provide assistance to the student.

13. Give directions in a variety of ways to increase the probability of understanding (e.g., if the student fails to understand verbal directions, present them in written form in order to ensure understanding).

14. Have the student repeat the directions orally to the teacher.

15. Give a signal (e.g., clapping hands, turning lights off and on, etc.) before giving verbal directions.

16. Provide the student with a predetermined signal when he/she is not beginning a task (e.g., turning lights off and on, hand signals, etc.).

17. Tell the student that directions will be given only once.

18. Rewrite directions at a lower reading level.

19. Deliver verbal directions in a more basic way.

20. Help the student with the first few items of a task and gradually reduce the amount of help over time.

21. Follow a less desirable task with a highly desirable task, making the completion of the first necessary to perform the second.

22. Provide the student with a schedule of activities in order that he/she will know exactly what and how much there is to do in a day.

23. Prevent the student from becoming overstimulated by an activity (e.g., frustrated, angry, etc.).

24. Specify exactly what is to be done for the completion of the task (e.g., make definite starting and stopping points, identify a minimum requirement, etc.).

25. Require the student to begin each assignment within a specified period of time (e.g., three minutes, five minutes, etc.).

26. Provide the student with shorter tasks given more frequently.

27. Provide the student with a selection of assignments and require him/her to choose a minimum number from the total (e.g., present the student with ten academic tasks from which he/she must finish six that day).

28. Start with a single direction and add more steps to the direction over time.

29. Provide the student with self-checking materials in order that he/she may check work privately, thus reducing the fear of public failure.

30. Have the student attempt a new assignment/activity in a private place (e.g., carrel, "office," quiet study area, etc.) in order to reduce the fear of public failure.

31. Have the student practice a new skill (e.g., jumping rope, dribbling a basketball) alone, with a peer, or with the teacher, before the entire group attempts the activity.

32. Allow the student the opportunity to perform the assignment/activity in a variety of ways (e.g., on tape, with a calculator, orally, etc.).

33. Deliver directions/instructions before handing out materials.

34. Allow the student to perform new assignments/activities in a variety of places in the building (e.g., resource room, library, learning center, etc.).

35. Provide the student with a sample of the assignment/activity which has been partially completed by a peer or teacher (e.g., book reports, projects).

36. Do not require the student to complete the assignment/activity in one sitting.

37. Allow the student the option of performing the assignment at another time (e.g., earlier in the day, later, another day).

38. Make certain that the student has all the materials he/she needs in order to perform the assignment/activity.

39. Have the student explain to the teacher what he/she thinks should be done in order to perform the assignment/activity.

40. Teach the student direction-following skills (e.g., listen carefully, write down important points, ask for clarification, wait until all directions are received before beginning).

41. Provide clearly stated directions, written or verbal (e.g., make the directions as simple and concrete as possible).

42. Interact frequently with the student in order to help him/her follow directions for the activity.

43. Structure the environment in such a way as to provide the student with increased opportunity for help or assistance on academic tasks (e.g., peer tutoring, the need for directions for work sent home, frequent interactions, etc.).

44. Provide alternatives to the traditional format for directions (e.g., tape record directions, summarize directions, directions given by peers, etc.).

45. Practice direction-following skills on nonacademic tasks.

46. Reduce the number of directions given at one time (e.g., give the student each additional step after completion of the previous step).

47. Make certain the student achieves success when following directions.

48. Establish assignment rules (e.g., listen to directions, wait until all directions have been given, ask questions about anything you do not understand, begin assignments only when you are certain about what is required, make certain you have all necessary materials).

49. Reinforce those students who receive directions before beginning a new task.

50. Require the student to wait until the teacher gives him/her a signal to begin (e.g., hand signal, ringing of bell, etc.).

51. Require the student to wait for other students to begin before he/she begins the task.

52. Require the student to have all necessary materials before beginning the task.

53. Allow the student access to pencils, pens, etc., only after directions have been given.

54. Make certain that the student is attending to the teacher (e.g., making eye contact, hands free of writing materials, looking at assignment, etc.) before giving directions.

55. Stand next to the student when giving directions.

56. Require the student to ask permission from the teacher to begin.

57. Maintain visibility to and from the student (e.g., the teacher should be able to see the student and the student should be able to see the teacher, making eye contact possible at all times) in order to make certain the student is attending.

58. Present directions following the outline of: (1) What, (2) How, (3) Materials, and (4) When.

59. Have the student take notes when directions are being given following the "What, How, Materials, and When" format. (See Appendix for Assignment Form.)

13 Does not follow multistep verbal directions

1. Provide clearly stated verbal directions (e.g., make the directions as simple and concrete as possible).

2. Help the student be successful with multistep directions (e.g., give verbal reminders, etc.), gradually reducing the amount of assistance given.

3. Provide verbal cues or signals to help the student recall steps.

4. Identify a peer to act as a model for the student to imitate following multistep verbal directions.

5. Assign a peer to work with the student to help him/her follow multistep verbal directions.

6. Carefully consider the student's age and ability before expecting him/her to follow multistep directions.

7. Present directions following the outline of: (1) What, (2) How, (3) Materials, and (4) When.

8. Have the student take notes when directions are being given following the "What, How, Materials, and When" format. (See Appendix for Assignment Form.)

9. Have the student practice following one-step directions. When he/she is successful, add a second step and have the student practice two-step directions until he/she is successful. Continue this process as the student develops the skills necessary to follow multistep directions.

10. Provide multistep directions in written form as well as verbal form for the student.

11. Deliver multistep directions to the student one step at a time. Gradually combine steps when giving directions as the student demonstrates success.

12. Have the student make notes for multistep directions, which he/she can then follow by reading the written form.

13. Reduce multistep verbal directions to fewer steps, gradually increasing expectations.

14. Communicate clearly to the student when it is time to listen to directions.

15. Make certain the student has all the materials necessary to perform all steps of the directions.

16. Make certain the student is attending to the teacher (e.g., making eye contact, looking at chalkboard, etc.) before giving multistep directions.

17. Provide the student with a written copy of the multistep directions.

18. Tape record multistep directions for the student to listen to individually and repeat as necessary.

19. Maintain consistency in the format in which verbal directions are given.

20. Have a peer help the student with any steps of the directions that he/she does not understand.

21. Seat the student close to the source of the verbal directions.

22. Work through the steps of the verbal directions as they are delivered in order to make certain the student follows the directions accurately.

23. Reduce distracting stimuli in order to increase the student's ability to follow verbal directions (e.g., place the student in the front row, provide a carrel or "office" space away from distractions, etc.). This is used as a means of reducing distracting stimuli and not as a form of punishment.

24. Interact frequently with the student in order to help him/her follow multistep verbal directions.

25. Provide alternatives for the traditional format of presenting verbal directions (e.g., tape record directions, summarize directions, directions given by peers, etc.).

26. Have the student practice following multi-step verbal directions for nonacademic tasks (e.g., recipes, games, etc.).

27. Have the student repeat or paraphrase multi-step verbal directions.

14 Has limited note-taking skills

1. Evaluate the appropriateness of note taking to determine: (a) if the task is too difficult, and (b) if the length of time scheduled to complete the task is appropriate.

2. Have the student question any directions, explanations, instructions he/she does not understand.

3. Teach the student to take notes in an early grade (i.e., third grade).

4. Teach the student to use the Outline Form (e.g., Who, What, Where, When, How, Why). The student should be required to practice this technique with attention given to note-taking skill development. (See Appendix for Outline Form.)

5. Teach the student to use the Mapping Form (e.g., Who, What, Where, When, How, Why). The student should be required to practice this technique with attention given to note-taking skill development. (See Appendix for Mapping Form.)

6. Teach the student to use the Double-Column Form (e.g., Who, What, Where, When, How, Why). The student should be required to practice this technique with attention given to note-taking skill development. (See Appendix for Double-Column Form.)

7. Teach the student to listen and look for key words (e.g., Christopher Columbus, Spain, New World, etc.).

8. Teach the student to listen and look for action words (e.g., sailed, discovered, founded, etc.).

9. Teach the student to listen and look for direction words (e.g., circle, underline, choose, list, etc.).

10. The teacher should practice pausing periodically during the lecture to allow students to fill in gaps and think about concepts presented.

11. Teach the student that it is acceptable to write notes in incomplete sentences.

12. Teach the student, when taking notes, to write the key words and main ideas that answer Who, What, Where, When, How, and Why. Students should then be given time periodically to go back to fill in connecting details (e.g., The student writes, "Christopher Columbus - Spain - New World - 1492," and is given time to go back to fill in "sailed from - to discover - during the year," resulting in a complete statement: "Christopher Columbus sailed from Spain to discover the New World during the year 1492.").

13. Teach the student to divide note-taking paper in the middle, writing main ideas and key words on the left side of the paper, filling in details and connecting points on the right side of the paper. These details and connecting points may be filled in after the lecture or during a pause.

14. Teach the student to learn and use abbreviations for words frequently used in order to take notes more effectively. Give the student the list of Selected Abbreviations and Symbols. (See Appendix.)

15. The teacher should give students several minutes at the end of a lecture to individually review their notes and ask questions to clarify points.

16. Assign the student a peer to work with to review notes at the end of each lecture. This teaches the student to clarify points and increases retention of material.

17. The teacher should require the student to review the previous day's notes for a short period of time before the new lecture.

18. Require the student to review lecture notes the first five minutes of each homework session (e.g., read notes silently, read notes orally, cover notes with a cover sheet and review from memory, etc.).

19. Have the student keep his/her notes organized in a folder for each subject or activity.

20. Teach the student to associate a known word or symbol with new information. This "association key" will serve to stimulate the student's memory.

21. The teacher should practice using several modalities when delivering a lecture (e.g., oral, written, overheads, etc.).

22. While delivering instructions, directions, lectures, etc., point out to the student that information should be written in the form of notes.

23. Check the student's notes before he/she begins an assignment in order to determine if they are correct and adequate for the assignment.

24. Provide the student with an outline or questions to be completed during teacher delivery of instructions, directions, lectures, etc.

25. Provide the student with samples of notes taken from actual instructions, directions, lectures, etc., given in the classroom in order that he/she may learn what information is necessary when taking notes.

26. Provide a standard format for lecture note taking (e.g., have paper and pencil or pen ready, listen for main ideas or important information, write a shortened form of main ideas or important information, ask to have any main ideas or important information repeated when necessary, etc.).

27. Make certain the student is in the best location in the classroom to receive information for note taking (e.g., near the board, teacher, or other source of information).

28. Make certain you can easily provide supervision of the student's note taking.

29. Make certain that instructions, directions, lectures, etc., are presented clearly and loudly enough for the student to hear.

30. Summarize the main points of instructions, directions, lectures, etc., for the student.

31. Make certain to maintain visibility to and from the student when delivering instructions, directions, lectures, etc., in order to enhance the likelihood of successful note taking.

32. Match the rate of delivery of instructions, directions, lectures, etc., to the student's ability to take notes.

33. Provide instructions, directions, lectures, etc., in sequential steps in order to enhance student note taking.

34. Provide delivery of information in short segments for the student to take notes. Gradually increase the length of delivery as the student experiences success in note taking.

35. Make certain that the vocabulary used in delivering instructions, directions, lectures, etc., is appropriate for the student's ability level.

36. Place the student next to a peer in order that the student can copy notes taken by the peer.

37. Make certain the student has all necessary materials for note taking (e.g., paper, pencil, pen, etc.).

38. Make certain the student has adequate surface space on which to write when taking notes (e.g., uncluttered desk top).

39. Reduce distracting stimuli that would interfere with the student's note taking (e.g., other students talking, outdoor activities, movement in the classroom, hallway noise, etc.).

40. Present the information in the most interesting manner possible.

41. As an alternative to note taking, have the student tape record instructions, directions, lectures, etc.

42. Make certain the student uses any necessary aids in order to facilitate note taking (e.g., eyeglasses, hearing aid, etc.).

15 Has limited memory skills

1. Use multiple modalities (e.g., auditory, visual, tactile, etc.) when presenting directions, explanations and instructional content.

2. Require the student to use a daily Assignment Sheet or Schedule of Daily Events to record assignments. (See Appendix.)

3. Require the student to use study aids when memorizing information (e.g., use flash card study aids, commercial flash cards, calculator, etc.).

4. Require the student to follow the recommended steps for studying. (See Appendix for Studying for a Test.)

5. Have the student write information he/she needs to remember in order to help the student develop a mental picture of the information.

6. Evaluate the appropriateness of the memory activities to determine: (a) if the task is too difficult, and (b) if the length of time scheduled to complete the task is appropriate.

7. Have the student question any directions, explanations, instructions he/she does not understand.

8. Have the student engage in concentration game activities with a limited number of symbols. Gradually increase the number of symbols as the student demonstrates success.

9. After a field trip or special event, have the student sequence the activities which occurred.

10. After reading a short story, have the student identify the main characters, sequence the events, and report the outcome of the story.

11. Record a message on tape. Have the student write the message after he/she has heard it. Increase the length of the message as the student demonstrates success.

12. Assign a peer tutor to engage in short-term memory activities with the student (e.g., concentration games, following directions, etc.).

13. Informally assess the student's auditory and visual short-term memory skills in order to determine which is the stronger. Utilize the results when presenting directions, explanations, and instructional content.

14. Teach the student how to organize information into smaller units (e.g., break the number sequence 132563 into units of 13, 25, 63).

15. Use sentence dictation to develop the student's short-term memory skills (e.g., begin with sentences of three words and increase the length of the sentences as the student demonstrates success).

16. Deliver directions, explanations, and instructional content in a clear manner and at an appropriate pace.

17. Have the student practice making notes for specific information he/she wants and/or needs to remember.

18. Teach the student to recognize key words and phrases related to information in order to increase his/her short-term or long-term memory skills.

19. Make certain the student is attending to the source of information (e.g., eye contact is being made, hands are free of materials, student is looking at assignment, etc.).

20. Reduce distracting stimuli when information is being presented, the student is studying, etc.

21. Stop at various points during the presentation of information to check the student's comprehension.

22. Have the student repeat/paraphrase directions, explanations, and instructions.

23. Provide the student with environmental cues and prompts designed to enhance his/her success in the classroom (e.g., posted rules, Schedule of Daily Events, steps for performing tasks, etc.). (See Appendix for Schedule of Daily Events.)

24. Provide the student with written lists of things to do, materials he/she will need, etc.

25. Teach the student to use associative cues or mnemonic devices to remember sequences.

26. Teach the student to recognize main points, important facts, etc. (See the Appendix for Outline Form.)

27. Assess the meaningfulness of the material to the student. Remembering is more likely to occur when the material is meaningful and the student can relate the material to real experiences.

28. Relate the information being presented to the student's previous experiences.

29. Help the student employ memory aids in order to recall words (e.g., a name might be linked to another word, for example, "Mr. Green is a very colorful person.").

30. Have the student outline, highlight, underline, or summarize information he/she should remember.

31. Make certain the student receives information from a variety of sources (e.g., texts, discussions, films, slide presentations, etc.) in order to enhance the student's memory/recall.

32. Have the student memorize the first sentence or line of poems, songs, etc. Require more to be memorized as the student experiences success.

33. Teach the student information-gathering skills (e.g., listen carefully, write down important points, ask for clarification, wait until all information is received before beginning, etc.).

34. Have the student be responsible for helping a peer remember sequences.

35. Use concrete examples and experiences in sharing information with the student.

36. Teach the student to recognize main points, important facts, etc. (See Appendix for Outline Form.)

37. When the student is required to recall information, provide him/her with auditory cues to help him/her remember the information (e.g., key words, a brief oral description to clue the student, etc.).

38. Make certain the student has adequate opportunities for repetition of information through different experiences in order to enhance his/her memory.

1. Provide the parents with specific instructions for how the student should study for tests/quizzes. (See Appendix for Studying for a Test.)

2. Provide the student with specific written instructions for what information will be included on a test (e.g., textbook pages, lecture material, charts, graphs, tables, etc.).

3. Require the student to record all information that will be included on tests/quizzes. (See Appendix for Assignment Form.)

4. Require the student to use a daily Assignment Sheet or Schedule of Daily Events in order to record assignments and dates of tests/quizzes. This is to insure early preparation for tests/quizzes. (See Appendix.)

5. Require the student to use the Outline Form when taking lecture notes. (See Appendix.)

6. Teach the student several note-taking strategies. Encourage the student to use the most effective strategy for him/her. (See Appendix for Outline Form, Mapping Form, Double-Column Form.)

7. Require the student to follow the steps when studying for a test. (See Appendix for Studying for a Test.)

8. Teach the student mnemonic memory strategies (e.g., to remember the Great Lakes have the student remember **HOMES** - Huron, Ontario, Michigan, Erie, Superior).

9. Identify a peer to act as a model for the student to imitate preparing for tests/quizzes.

10. Have the student question any directions, explanations, instructions he/she does not understand.

11. Provide the student with a list of necessary materials required in order to be prepared for tests/quizzes.

12. Give the student a practice test in class.

13. Provide the student with verbal reminders of materials required in order to be prepared for tests/quizzes.

14. At the end of the day, remind the student which materials are required for tests/quizzes to be given the next day (e.g., send a note home, verbal reminder, etc.).

15. Provide the student with structure for all tests/quizzes (e.g., specific directions, routine format for tests/quizzes, time units, etc.).

16. Provide the student with adequate time at school to prepare for assigned tests/quizzes (e.g., supervised study time).

17. Assign a peer tutor to work with the student in order to prepare him/her for assigned tests/quizzes.

18. Reduce the number/length of tests/quizzes. Gradually increase the number/length of tests/quizzes as the student demonstrates success.

19. Provide the student with written directions to follow in preparing for all assigned tests/quizzes.

20. Provide individual assistance to the student in order to help him/her prepare for assigned tests/quizzes (e.g., time set aside during the day, during study hall, after school, etc.).

21. Identify other personnel in the school who may assist the student in preparing for assigned tests/quizzes (e.g., aide, librarian, other teachers, etc.).

22. Provide a review session in which test topics and typical questions are covered.

23. Have the student study for tests according to the "Who, What, Where, When, How and Why" format. The teacher should then test on this information. (See Appendix for Outline Form.)

24. Require the student to check all answers on tests for accuracy.

25. Provide the student with multiple opportunities to master what will be covered by the test (e.g., listening to presentations in class; reading assigned materials; studying with a friend; playing games over the test material, such as *Jeopardy*; etc.).

26. Provide the student with sample questions from the test.

27. Present concepts following the outline of: (1) Who, (2) What, (3) Where, (4) When, (5) How, and (6) Why.

17 Has limited test-taking skills

1. Make sure the reading level is appropriate for the student.

2. Make sure directions are completely understood by the student (e.g., have the student paraphrase the directions).

3. Require the student to read all multiple-choice answers before responding.

4. On true-false items, have the student underline key words before responding.

5. On true-false items, teach the student that, in order for an item to be true, the whole statement must be true.

6. On matching items, teach the student to read all choices prior to responding.

7. On matching items, teach the student to respond to known items first, marking off used responses.

8. Teach the student to pace himself/herself on timed tests.

9. For standardized bubble-format tests, require the student to use a place marker on the response sheet.

10. Teach the student mnemonic devices to remember information.

11. Require the student to list important points prior to the test as a pretest.

12. For spelling tests, have the student write spelling words five times each while saying them aloud.

13. For spelling tests, have the student take a pre-test one day prior to the test.

14. Teach the student not to spend too much time on any one item on timed tests.

15. Teach the student to proofread all items on a test.

16. On essay tests, have the student include Who, What, Where, When, How, and Why in the answer.

17. Give the student a practice test in class.

18. Have the student study with a peer.

19. Allow the student to take the test in another place in the building (e.g., resource room, counselor's office, etc.).

20. Allow the student additional time to take the test.

21. Provide the student with sample questions from the test.

22. Make certain the student knows what topic/areas will be covered by the test.

23. Provide a review session in which test topics and typical questions are covered.

24. Require the student to check all answers on tests for accuracy.

25. Allow the student to take the test orally (i.e., read the test to the student with the student responding orally).

26. For standardized tests, give the student sample test questions in order that he/she may become comfortable with the format.

27. Have the student study for tests according to the Who, What, Where, When, How, and Why format; then test according to that same information.

28. Provide time for the student to study for tests at school rather than home.

29. Provide the student with multiple opportunities to master what will be covered by the test (e.g., listening to presentations in class; reading assigned materials; studying with a friend; playing games over the test material, such as *Jeopardy*; etc.).

18 Has limited task focus and task completion

1. Evaluate the appropriateness of the task to determine: (a) if the task is too difficult, and (b) if the length of time scheduled for the task is appropriate.

2. Assign a peer to help the student with class assignments.

3. Assess the degree of task difficulty in comparison with the student's ability to perform the task.

4. Assign the student shorter tasks (e.g., modify a 20-problem math activity to 4 activities of 5 problems each, to be done at various times during the day). Gradually increase the length of the task over time.

5. Present tasks in the most attractive and interesting manner possible.

6. Reduce distracting stimuli (e.g., place the student in the front row, provide a carrel or quiet place away from distractions). This is used as a means of reducing stimuli and not as a form of punishment.

7. Interact frequently with the student in order to maintain involvement with class assignments (e.g., ask the student questions, ask the student's opinion, stand close to the student, seat the student near the teacher's desk, etc.).

8. Allow the student additional time to complete class assignments.

9. Supervise the student during class assignments in order to maintain on-task behavior.

10. Deliver directions orally in order to increase the probability of the student's understanding of class assignments.

11. Make certain the student understands the natural consequences of failing to complete assignments (e.g., students who do not finish their work will not get to do more desirable activities).

12. Repeat directions in order to increase the probability of understanding.

13. Encourage the student to ask for clarification of directions for classroom assignments.

14. Follow a less desirable task with a highly desirable task, making the completion of the first necessary to perform the second.

15. Give directions in a variety of ways to increase the probability of understanding (e.g., if the student fails to understand verbal directions, present them in written form).

16. Provide the student with step-by-step written directions for class assignments.

17. Allow the student to perform alternative assignments. Gradually introduce more components of the regular assignments until those assignments are routinely performed.

18. Maintain consistency of expectations while keeping expectations within the ability level of the student.

19. Allow the student the option of performing the assignment at another time (e.g., earlier in the day, later in the day, on another day, or later at home).

20. Provide the student with a selection of assignments and require him/her to choose a minimum number from the total amount (e.g., present the student with ten academic tasks from which he/she must finish six that day).

21. Maintain mobility in order to be frequently near the student to provide cues and prompts to assist the student in performing classroom assignments.

22. Communicate with parents (e.g., notes home, phone calls, etc.) in order to share information concerning the student's progress and so that they may reinforce the student at home for completing assignments at school.

23. Modify the task assignment in order that the student will be able to complete the assignment during class time (e.g., individualize spelling lists by matching lists to the student's ability level).

24. Teach the student basic study skills (e.g., finding key words and phrases; underlining or highlighting important facts; identifying "Who, What, Where, When, How, and Why"; etc.).

25. Teach direction-following skills (e.g., key words in directions; use of sequential words in directions in order to perform steps such as *first, then, next*; etc.).

26. Have the student take notes when directions are being given following the "What, How, Materials, and When" format. (See Appendix for Assignment Form.)

27. Present assignments following the outline of: (1) What, (2) How, (3) Materials, and (4) When.

28. Maintain consistency in the daily routine.

29. Work a few problems with the student on an assignment in order to serve as a model and help the student begin a task.

30. Reinforce the student for beginning, staying on, and completing assignments.

31. Identify a peer to act as a model for the student to imitate appropriate completion of assignments.

32. Have the student question any directions, explanations, instructions he/she does not understand.

33. Assess the quality and clarity of directions, explanations, and instructions given to the student.

34. Structure the environment in such a way as to provide the student with increased opportunity for help or assistance (e.g., seat the student close to the teacher's desk, seat the student near a peer who can provide assistance, etc.).

35. Communicate clearly to the student the length of time he/she has to complete the assignment.

36. Communicate clearly to the student when the assignment should be completed.

37. Have the student time his/her assignments in order to monitor his/her own behavior and accept time limits.

38. Structure time units in order that the student knows exactly how long he/she has to work and when he/she must be finished.

39. Provide the student with more than enough time to finish an activity and decrease the amount of time as the student demonstrates success.

40. Have the student repeat the directions orally to the teacher.

41. Provide the student with a Schedule of Daily Events in order that he/she knows exactly what and how much there is to do in a day. (See Appendix.)

42. Prevent the student from becoming over-stimulated by an activity (e.g., frustrated, angry, etc.).

43. Specify exactly what is to be done for the completion of the task (e.g., indicate definite starting and stopping points, indicate a minimum requirement, etc.).

44. Require the student to begin each assignment within a specified period of time (e.g., three minutes, five minutes, etc.).

45. Provide the student with shorter tasks given more frequently.

46. Provide clearly stated directions in written or verbal form (i.e., make the directions as simple and concrete as possible).

47. Interact frequently with the student in order to help him/her follow directions for the assignments.

48. Provide alternatives for the traditional format of directions (e.g., tape record directions, summarize directions, directions given by peers, etc.).

49. Practice direction-following skills on nonacademic tasks.

50. Reduce directions to steps (e.g., give the student each additional step after completion of the previous step).

51. Make certain the student achieves success when following directions.

52. Reduce the emphasis on early completion. Hurrying to complete assignments may cause the student to fail to follow directions.

53. Establish assignment rules (e.g., listen to directions, wait until all directions have been given, ask questions about anything you do not understand, begin an assignment only when you are certain about what you are supposed to do, make certain you have all necessary materials, etc.).

54. Allow the student access to pencils, pens, etc., only after directions have been given.

55. Make certain that the student is attending to the teacher when directions are given (e.g., making eye contact, hands free of writing materials, looking at assignment, etc.).

56. Maintain visibility to and from the student in order to make certain the student is attending. The teacher should be able to see the student and the student should be able to see the teacher, making eye contact possible at all times.

57. Present one assignment at a time. As each assignment is completed, deliver reinforcement along with the presentation of the next assignment.

58. Have the student use a timer in order to complete tasks within a given period of time.

59. Provide the student with the opportunity to perform assignments/activities in a variety of ways (e.g., on tape, with a calculator, orally, etc.).

60. Have the student explain to the teacher what he/she should do in order to perform the assignments.

61. Make certain that the reading demands of the assignment are within the ability level of the student.

62. Read directions, explanations, and instructions to the student when necessary.

63. Use a sight word vocabulary approach in order to teach the student key words and phrases when reading directions and instructions (e.g., key words such as *circle, underline, match*, etc.).

64. Shorten the length of assignments in order that the student can complete his/her assignments in the same length of time as other students.

65. Provide the student with additional time to complete assignments if necessary, in order for the student to be successful.

66. When testing, make certain the student's knowledge of content is being assessed rather than the student's ability to read directions, instructions, and information.

67. Maintain mobility in order to be frequently near the student and to provide reading assistance.

68. Have the student practice timed drills consisting of reading directions, explanations, information, etc., in order to reduce reading time.

69. Keep written directions as concise and concrete as possible.

70. Provide the student with a copy of written directions at his/her desk rather than on the chalkboard, posted in the classroom, etc.

71. Seat the student close to the source of written information (e.g., chalkboard, projector, etc.).

72. Make certain that the print is large enough to increase the student's likelihood of success.

73. Gradually increase the degree of difficulty or complexity of written directions, explanations, instructions, information, etc., as the student becomes more successful.

74. Modify or rewrite the reading level of material presented to the student.

75. Reduce the emphasis on competition. Competitive activities may make it difficult for the student to finish assignments because of frustration with reading difficulties.

76. Reinforce the student for attempting and completing assignments based on the amount of work he/she can successfully complete. Gradually increase the amount of work required for reinforcement as the student demonstrates success.

77. Provide the student a quiet place (e.g., carrel, study booth, etc.) where he/she may go to engage in reading activities.

78. Write a contract with the student specifying what behavior is expected (e.g., attempting and completing class assignments) and what reinforcement will be made available when the terms of the contract have been met.

79. Communicate with parents (e.g., notes home, phone calls, etc.) in order to share information concerning the student's progress and so that they may reinforce the student at home for finishing assignments at school.

80. Reinforce the student for finishing assignments within a length of time which is reasonable for him/her. Gradually reduce the length of time the student has to complete assignments as he/she demonstrates success.

81. Tape record directions, explanations, and instructions in order to enhance the student's success.

82. Have a peer read directions, explanations, and instructions to the student in order to enhance the student's success.

83. Require the student to verbally repeat directions, explanations, and instructions he/she has read.

19 Is unable to perform assignments independently

1. Make certain that directions, explanations, and instructions are delivered on the student's ability level.

2. Work a few problems of an assignment with the student in order to serve as a model and help the student begin a task.

3. Have the student keep a chart or graph representing the number of assignments he/she completes independently.

4. Reinforce the student for performing assignments independently: (a) give the student a tangible reward (e.g., classroom privileges, line leading, passing out materials, five minutes free time, etc.) when he/she performs assignments independently, or (b) give the student an intagible reward (e.g., praise, handshake, smile, etc.) for performing assignments independently.

5. Establish classroom rules (e.g., work on task, work quietly, remain in your seat, finish task, meet task expectations).   Reiterate rules often and reinforce students for following rules.

6. Reinforce those students in the classroom who perform assignments independently.

7. Assess the degree of task difficulty in comparison with the student's ability to perform the task.

8. Assign the student shorter tasks (e.g., modify a 20-problem math activity to 4 activities of 5 problems each, to be done at various times during the day). Gradually increase the number of problems as the student demonstrates success.

9. Present the task in the most interesting manner possible.

10. Reduce distracting stimuli (e.g., place the student in the front row, provide a carrel or quiet place away from distractions, etc.). This is to be used as a means of reducing distracting stimuli and not as a form of punishment.

11. Allow the student additional time to complete assignments when working independently.

12. Provide the student with step-by-step written directions for performing assignments.

13. Allow the student to perform alternative assignments. Gradually introduce more components of the regular assignments until those assignments are routinely performed.

14. Maintain consistency of expectations while keeping expectations within the ability level of the student.

15. Have a peer work a few problems with the student on an assignment in order to serve as a model and help the student begin a task.

16. Maintain consistency in daily routine.

17. Allow the student to use materials that will assist him/her in performing assignments independently (e.g., calculator, manipulatives, flash cards, etc.).

18. Provide the student with a predetermined nonverbal signal or cue to stimulate the student to begin independent assignments (e.g., place hand on shoulder, make eye contact, etc.).

19. Structure the environment in such a way as to provide the student with increased opportunity for help or assistance (e.g., seat the student close to the teacher's desk).

20. Have the student take notes when directions are being given following the "What, How, Materials, and When" format. (See Appendix for Assignment Form.)

21. Present directions following the outline of: (1) What, (2) How, (3) Materials, and (4) When.

22. Reinforce the student for beginning, working on, and completing assignments.

23. Speak to the student to explain: (a) what he/she is doing wrong (e.g., not performing assignments independently) and (b) what he/she should be doing (e.g., performing assignments independently).

24. Reinforce the student for performing assignments independently based on the number of times he/she can be successful. Gradually increase the number of times required for reinforcement as the student demonstrates success.

25. Write a contract with the student specifying what behavior is expected (e.g., performing assignments independently) and what reinforcement will be made available when the terms of the contract have been met.

26. Communicate with parents, agencies or appropriate parties in order to inform them of the problem, determine the cause of the problem, and find solutions to the problem.

27. Identify a peer to act as a model for the student to imitate independent completion of assignments.

28. Encourage the student to question any directions, explanations, instructions he/she does not understand.

29. Evaluate the appropriateness of expecting the student to complete assignments independently.

30. Maintain mobility throughout the classroom in order to determine the student's needs.

31. Frequently offer the student assistance throughout the day.

32. In order to detect the student's needs, communicate with the student as often as opportunities permit.

33. Communicate with parents (e.g., notes home, phone calls, etc.) in order to share information concerning the student's progress and so that they may reinforce the student at home for performing assignments independently.

20 Performs classroom tests or quizzes at a failing level

1. Evaluate the appropriateness of the task to determine: (a) if the task is too difficult, and (b) if the length of time scheduled for the task is appropriate.

2. Have the student question anything he/she does not understand while taking tests or quizzes.

3. Make certain that the tests or quizzes measure knowledge of content and not related skills, such as reading or writing.

4. Teach the student test-taking strategies (e.g., answer questions you are sure of first, learn to summarize, recheck each answer, etc.). (See Appendix for Test-Taking Skills.)

5. Give shorter tests or quizzes, but give them more frequently. Increase the length of tests or quizzes over time as the student demonstrates success.

6. Have tests or quizzes read to the student.

7. Have the student answer tests or quizzes orally.

8. Have the tests or quizzes tape recorded and allow the student to listen to questions as often as necessary.

9. Allow the student to take tests or quizzes in a quiet place in order to reduce distractions (e.g., study carrel, library, resource room, etc.).

10. Have the student take tests or quizzes in the resource room where the resource teacher can clarify questions, offer explanations, etc.

11. Provide the student with opportunities for review before taking tests or quizzes.

12. Have the student maintain a performance record for each subject in which he/she is experiencing difficulty.

13. Teach and encourage the student to practice basic study skills (e.g., reading for the main point, taking notes, summarizing, highlighting, studying in an appropriate environment, using time wisely, etc.) before taking tests or quizzes.

14. Assess student performance in a variety of ways (e.g., have the student give verbal explanations, simulations, physical demonstrations of a skill, etc.).

15. Arrange a time for the student to study with a peer tutor before taking tests or quizzes.

16. Provide a variety of opportunities for the student to learn the information covered by tests or quizzes (e.g., films, visitors, community resources, etc.).

17. Allow the student to respond to alternative test or quiz questions (e.g., more generalized questions which represent global understanding).

18. Provide the opportunity for the student to study daily assignments with a peer.

19. Have the student take a sample test or quiz before the actual test.

20. Remove the threat of public knowledge of failure (e.g., test or quiz results are not read aloud or posted, test ranges are not made public, etc.).

21. Provide parents with information on test and quiz content (e.g., the material that will be covered by the test or quiz, the format, the types of questions, etc.).

22. Modify instruction to include more concrete examples in order to enhance student learning.

23. Monitor student performance in order to detect errors and determine where learning problems exist.

24. Reduce the emphasis on competition. Students who compete academically and fail may cease to try to succeed and do far less than they are capable of achieving.

25. Only give tests and quizzes when the student is certain to succeed (e.g., after he/she has learned the information).

26. Make certain that the test questions are worded exactly as the information was given in either verbal or written form.

27. Prior to the test, provide the student with all information that will be on the test (e.g., "You will need to know . . ." and list those items).

28. Provide the student with a set of prepared notes that summarize the material to be tested.

29. Have the student listen and take notes for the "Who, What, Where, When, How, and Why" while concepts are presented. (See Appendix for Outline Form.)

30. Present concepts following the outline of: (1) Who, (2) What, (3) Where, (4) When, (5) How, and (6) Why.

31. Have the student prepare for tests using the "Who, What, Where, When, How, and Why" system. (See Appendix for Outline Form.)

32. Develop tests and quizzes for the student using the "Who, What, Where, When, How, and Why" approach.

33. Teach the student skills to use when taking tests. (See Appendix for Test-Taking Skills.)

34. Review with the student the "Additional Suggestions" located in the Appendix under Test-Taking Skills.

35. Teach the student skills for studying for tests/quizzes. (See Appendix for Studying for a Test.)

36. Review with the student the "Additional Suggestions" located in the Appendix under Studying for a Test.

37. Teach the student skills to use when taking notes. (See Appendix for Note Taking.)

38. Speak with the student to explain: (a) what he/she is doing wrong (e.g., not attending in class, not using study time, etc.) and (b) what he/she should be doing (e.g., attending during class, asking questions, using study time, etc.).

39. Write a contract with the student specifying what behavior is expected (e.g., improved test or quiz scores) and what reinforcement will be made available when the terms of the contract have been met.

40. Communicate with the parents (e.g., notes home, phone calls, etc.) in order to share information concerning the student's progress and so that they may reinforce the student at home for improved test or quiz scores.

21 Does not perform academically at his/her ability level

1. Write a contract with the student specifying what behavior is expected (e.g., completing an assignment with _____% accuracy) and what reinforcement will be made available when the terms of the contract have been met.

2. Communicate with parents (e.g., notes home, phone calls, etc.) in order to share information concerning the student's progress and so that they may reinforce the student at home for improving his/her academic task and homework performance.

3. Evaluate the appropriateness of the task to determine: (a) if the task is too difficult, and (b) if the length of time scheduled to complete the task is appropriate.

4. Have the student question any directions, explanations, instructions he/she does not understand.

5. Assess student performance in a variety of ways (e.g., have the student give verbal explanations, simulations, physical demonstrations, etc.).

6. Give shorter assignments, but give them more frequently. Increase the length of the assignments as the student demonstrates success.

7. Structure the environment in such a way as to provide the student with increased opportunity for help or assistance on academic or homework tasks (e.g., provide a peer tutor, seat the student near the teacher or aide, etc.).

8. Have the student listen and take notes for the "Who, What, Where, When, How, and Why" while concepts are presented. (See Appendix for Outline Form.)

9. Present concepts following the outline of: (1) Who, (2) What, (3) Where, (4) When, (5) How, and (6) Why.

10. Have the student prepare for tests using the "Who, What, Where, When, How, and Why" system. (See Appendix for Outline Form.)

11. Develop tests and quizzes for the student using the "Who, What, Where, When, How, and Why" approach.

12. Teach the student study skills (i.e., organization, test-taking skills, etc.). (See Appendix for Studying for a Test.)

13. Reduce distracting stimuli (e.g., place the student in the front row, provide a carrel or "office" space away from distractions, etc.). This is used as a means of reducing distracting stimuli and not as a form of punishment.

14. Interact frequently with the student to monitor his/her task performance.

15. Have the student maintain a chart representing the number of tasks completed and the accuracy rate of each task.

16. Provide time at school for the completion of homework if assigned homework has not been completed or has resulted in failure. (The student's failure to complete homework assignments may be the result of variables in the home over which he/she has no control.)

17. Assess the appropriateness of assigning homework to the student.

18. Teach the student note-taking skills.

19. Teach the student direction-following skills: (a) listen carefully, (b) ask questions, (c) use environmental cues, (d) rely on examples provided, etc.

20. Identify resource personnel from whom the student may receive additional assistance (e.g., librarian, special educational teacher, other personnel with expertise or time to help, etc.).

21. Establish a level of minimum accuracy which will be accepted as a level of mastery.

22. Deliver reinforcement for any and all measures of improvement.

23. Mastery should not be expected too soon after introducing new information, skills, etc.

24. Provide the student with self-checking materials, requiring correction before turning in assignments.

25. Should the student consistently fail to complete assignments with minimal accuracy, evaluate the appropriateness of tasks assigned.

26. Provide instruction and task format in a variety of ways (e.g., verbal instructions, written instructions, demonstrations, simulations, manipulatives, drill activities with peers, etc.).

27. If the student has difficulty completing homework assignments with minimal accuracy, provide a time during the day when he/she can receive assistance at school.

28. Make certain the assignments measure knowledge of content and not related skills such as reading or writing.

29. Have assignments read to the student.

30. Have the student respond to tasks orally.

31. Have the assignments tape recorded, allowing the student to listen to questions as often as necessary.

32. Have the student perform difficult assignments in the resource room where the resource teacher can answer questions.

33. Provide the student with opportunities for review prior to grading assignments.

34. Teach the student to practice basic study skills (e.g., reading for the main idea, taking notes, summarizing, highlighting, studying in a good environment, using time wisely, etc.).

35. Arrange a time for the student to study with a peer tutor before completing a graded assignment.

36. Allow the student to respond to alternative assignment questions (e.g., more generalized questions that represent global understanding).

37. Provide parents with information regarding appropriate ways in which to help their child with homework (e.g., read directions with the student, work a few problems together, answer questions, check the completed assignment, etc.).

38. Modify instruction to include more concrete examples in order to enhance student learning.

39. Monitor student performance in order to detect errors and determine where learning problems exist.

40. Reduce the emphasis on competition. Students who compete academically and fail to succeed may cease to try to do well and do far less than they are able.

41. Allow/require the student to make corrections after assignments have been checked the first time.

42. Provide the student with evaluative feedback for assignments completed (i.e., identify what the student did successfully, what errors were made, and what should be done to correct the errors).

43. Maintain consistency in assignment format and expectations so as not to confuse the student.

44. Provide adequate repetition and drill to assure minimal accuracy of assignments presented (i.e., require mastery/minimal accuracy before moving to the next skill level).

45. It is not necessary to grade every assignment performed by the student. Assignments may be used to evaluate student ability or knowledge and provide feedback. Grades may not need to be assigned until mastery/minimal accuracy has been attained.

46. Allow the student to put an assignment away and return to it as a later time if he/she could be more successful.

47. Provide the student with a selection of assignments and require him/her to choose a minimum number from the total amount (e.g., present the student with ten academic tasks from which he/she must finish six that day).

48. Have the student practice an assignment with the teacher, aide, or peer before performing the assignment for a grade.

49. Monitor the first problem or part of the assignment in order to make certain the student knows what is expected of him/her.

50. Provide frequent interactions and encouragement to support the student's confidence and optimism for success (e.g., make statements such as, "You're doing great." "Keep up the good work." "You should be proud of yourself." etc.).

51. Build varying degrees of difficulty into assignments in order to insure the student's self-confidence and at the same time provide a challenge (e.g., easier problems are intermingled with problems designed to measure knowledge gained).

52. Work the first few problems of an assignment with the student in order to make certain that he/she knows what to do, how to perform the assignment, etc.

53. Modify academic tasks (e.g., format, requirements, length, etc.).

54. Provide the student with clearly stated step-by-step directions for homework in order that someone at home may be able to provide assistance.

55. Make certain that homework relates to concepts already taught rather than introducing a new concept.

56. Have a peer work a few problems with the student on an assignment in order to serve as a model and help the student begin a task.

57. Allow the student to use materials that will assist him/her in performing assignments independently (e.g., calculator, manipulatives, flash cards, etc.).

Please note: If the student continues to fail in spite of the above interventions and is not being served by special education personnel, he/she should be considered for referral for special education.

1. Make certain that written directions are presented on the student's reading level.

2. Maintain consistency in the format of written directions.

3. Transfer directions from texts and workbooks when pictures or other stimuli make it difficult to attend to or follow written directions.

4. Highlight, circle, or underline key words in written directions (e.g., key words such as *match, circle, underline,* etc.).

5. Evaluate the appropriateness of the task to determine: (a) if the task is too difficult, and (b) if the length of time scheduled to complete the task is appropriate.

6. Identify a peer to act as a model for the student to imitate appropriate following of written directions.

7. Have the student question any written directions, explanations, instructions he/she does not understand.

8. Assign a peer to work with the student to help him/her follow written directions.

9. Teach the student the skills of following written directions (e.g., read carefully, write down important points, ask for clarification, wait until all directions are received before beginning, etc.).

10. Give directions in a variety of ways to increase the probability of understanding (e.g., if the student fails to understand written directions, present them in verbal form).

11. Provide clearly stated written directions (e.g., make the directions as simple and concrete as possible).

12. Interact frequently with the student in order to help him/her follow written directions.

13. Reduce distracting stimuli in order to increase the student's ability to follow written directions (e.g., place the student on the front row, provide a carrel or "office" space away from distractions, etc.). This is used as a means of reducing distracting stimuli and not as a form of punishment.

14. Structure the environment in such a way as to provide the student with increased opportunity for help or assistance on academic tasks (e.g., peer tutoring, directions for work sent home, frequent interactions, etc.).

15. Provide alternatives for the traditional format of presenting written directions (e.g., tape record directions, summarize directions, directions given by peers, etc.).

16. Assess the quality and clarity of written directions, explanations, and instructions given to the student.

17. Practice the following of written directions on nonacademic tasks (e.g., recipes, games, etc.).

18. Have the student repeat written directions orally to the teacher.

19. Reduce written directions to individual steps (e.g., give the student each additional step after completion of the previous step).

20. Deliver a predetermined signal (e.g., clapping hands, turning lights off and on, etc.) before giving written directions.

21. Deliver written directions before handing out materials.

22. Make certain the student achieves success when following written directions.

23. Reduce the emphasis on competition. Competitive activities may cause the student to hurry to begin the task without following written directions.

24. Require the student to wait until the teacher gives him/her a signal to begin an activity after receiving written directions (e.g., hand signal, bell ringing, etc.).

25. Make certain that the student is attending to the teacher (e.g., eye contact, hand free of writing materials, looking at assignment, etc.) before giving written directions.

26. Maintain visibility to and from the student. The teacher should be able to see the student and the student should be able to see the teacher, making eye contact possible at all times in order to make certain the student is attending to written directions.

27. Present directions in both written and verbal form.

28. Provide the student with a copy of written directions at his/her desk rather than on the chalkboard, posted in the classroom, etc.

29. Tape record directions for the student to listen to individually and repeat as necessary.

30. Develop assignments/activities requiring the following of written directions (e.g., informal activities designed to have the student carry out directions in steps, increasing the degree of difficulty).

31. Have a peer help the student with any written directions he/she does not understand.

32. Seat the student close to the source of the written directions.

33. Make certain that the print is large enough to increase the likelihood of following the written directions.

34. Work the first problem or problems with the student to make certain that he/she follows the written directions.

35. Work through the steps of written directions as they are delivered in order to make certain the student follows the directions accurately.

36. Have the student carry out written directions one step at a time, checking with the teacher to make certain that each step is successfully followed before attempting the next.

37. Make certain that directions are given at the level at which the student can be successful (e.g., two-step or three-step directions should not be given to students who can only successfully follow one-step directions).

38. Use visual cues such as *green dot* to start, *red dot* to stop, arrows, etc., in written directions.

39. Provide the beginning reader with written directions supplemented with rebus clues, gradually phasing out the rebus clues.

40. Teach a sight word vocabulary of direction words such as *circle, fill-in, match.*

41. Keep written directions as concise and concrete as possible.

42. Gradually increase the degree of difficulty or complexity of written directions, explanations, instructions, information, etc., as the student becomes more successful.

43. Have the student take notes when directions are being given following the "What, How, Materials, and When" format. (See Appendix for Assisgnment Form.)

44. Present directions following the outline of: (1) What, (2) How, (3) Materials, and (4) When. (See Appendix for Assignment Form.)

23 Requires repeated drill and practice to learn what other students master easily

1. Reduce the emphasis on competition. Competitive activities may cause the student to hurry and make mistakes.

2. Give the student fewer concepts to learn at any one time, spending more time on each concept until the student learns it correctly.

3. Have a peer spend time each day engaged in drill activities with the student.

4. Have the student use new concepts frequently throughout the day.

5. Have the student highlight or underline key words, phrases and sentences from reading assignments, newspapers, magazines, etc.

6. Develop crossword puzzles which contain only the student's spelling words and have him/her complete them.

7. Write sentences, passages, paragraphs, etc., for the student to read which reinforce new concepts.

8. Have the student act as a peer tutor to teach concepts just learned to another student.

9. Have the student review new concepts each day for a short period of time rather than two or three times per week for longer periods of time.

10. Use wall charts to introduce new concepts with visual images, such as pictures for the student to associate with previously learned concepts.

11. Initiate a "learn a concept a day" program with the student and incorporate the concept into the assigned activities for the day.

12. Require the student to use resources (e.g., encyclopedia, dictionary, etc.) to provide information to help him/her be successful when performing tasks.

13. Allow the student to use devices to help him/her successfully perform tasks (e.g., calculator, multiplication tables, abacus, dictionary, etc.).

14. Provide the student with times throughout the day when he/she can engage in drill activities with the teacher, an aide, a peer, etc.

15. Provide the student with opportunities for drill activities in the most interesting manner possible (e.g., working with the computer, using a calculator, playing educational games, watching a film, listening to a tape, etc.).

16. Give the student a list of key words, phrases, or main points to learn for each new concept introduced.

17. Underline, circle, or highlight important information from any material the student is to learn (e.g., science, math, geography, etc.).

18. Provide the student with the information he/she needs to learn in the most direct manner possible (e.g., a list of facts, a summary of important points, an outline of important events, etc.).

19. Tape record important information the student can listen to as often as necessary.

20. Obtain computer software which provides repeated drill of general concepts and facts.

21. Obtain computer software which has the capability of programming the student's individual spelling words, facts, etc., for repeated drill and practice.

22. Encourage the student to review new concepts each evening for a short period of time.

23. Use concrete examples in teaching the student new information and concepts.

24. Break the sequence into units and have the student learn one unit at a time.

25. Make certain the student has adequate opportunities for repetition of information through different experiences in order to enhance his/her memory.

26. Make certain the student receives information from a variety of sources (e.g., texts, discussions, films, etc.) in order to enhance the student's memory/recall.

27. When a student is required to recall information, remind him/her of the situation in which the material was originally presented (e.g., "Remember when we talked about . . ." etc.).

28. Have the student listen and take notes for the "Who, What, Where, When, How, and Why" while concepts are presented. (See Appendix for Outline Form.)

29. Present concepts following the outline of: (1) Who, (2) What, (3) Where, (4) When, (5) How, and (6) Why.

30. Have the student prepare for tests using the "Who, What, Where, When, How, and Why" system. (See Appendix for Outline Form.)

31. Develop tests and quizzes for the student using the "Who, What, Where, When, How, and Why" approach.

24 Has difficulty retrieving or recalling concepts, persons, places, etc.

1. Have the student act as a classroom messenger. Give the student a verbal message to deliver to another teacher, secretary, administrator, etc. Increase the length of messages as the student is successful.

2. At the end of the school day, have the student recall three activities in which he/she participated during the day. Gradually increase the number of activities the student is required to recall as he/she demonstrates success.

3. After a field trip or special event, have the student recall the activities which occurred.

4. After reading a short story, have the student recall the main characters, sequence the events, and recall the outcome of the story.

5. Help the student employ memory aids or mnemonic devices in order to recall words (e.g., a name might be linked to another word, for example, "Mr. Green is a very colorful person.").

6. Encourage the student to play word games such as *Hangman, Concentration, Password,* etc.

7. Have the student compete against himself/herself by timing how fast he/she can name a series of pictured objects. The student tries to increase his/her speed each time.

8. Have the student take notes from classes, presentations, lectures, etc., to help him/her facilitate recall.

9. Have the student make notes, lists, etc., of things he/she needs to be able to recall. The student carries these reminders with him/her.

10. Have the student tape record important information he/she should remember.

11. Have the student outline, highlight, underline, or summarize information he/she should remember.

12. Make certain the student has adequate opportunities for repetition of information through different experiences in order to enhance his/her memory.

13. When the student is required to recall information, remind him/her of the situation in which the material was originally presented (e.g., "Remember yesterday when we talked about . . ." "Remember when we were outside and I told you about the . . ." etc.).

14. Have the student practice repetition of information in order to increase accurate memory skills (e.g., repeating names, telephone numbers, dates of events, etc.).

15. Show the student an object or a picture of an object for a few seconds. Ask the student to recall specific attributes of the object (e.g., color, size, shape, etc.).

16. Teach the student to recognize key words and phrases related to information in order to increase his/her memory skills.

17. Make certain the student receives information from a variety of sources (e.g., texts, discussions, films, slide presentations, etc.) in order to enhance the student's memory/recall.

18. Provide the student with verbal cues to stimulate recall of material previously presented (e.g., key words, a brief oral description, etc.).

19. Teach concepts through associative learning (e.g., build new concepts based on previous learning).

20. Encourage the student to use semantic mapping techniques in order to stimulate visual memory.

21. Provide opportunities for overlearning material presented, in order for the student to be able to recall the information.

22. Have the student use a Schedule of Daily Events to recall assignments to be reviewed. (See Appendix.)

23. Evaluate the appropriateness of the information to be recalled to determine: (a) if the task is too difficult, and (b) if the length of time scheduled to complete the task is appropriate.

24. Use multiple modalities (e.g., auditory, visual, tactile, etc.) when presenting instructional content.

25. Have a peer tutor engage in memory activities with the student (e.g., concentration games, flash cards, math facts, etc.).

26. Teach the student how to organize information into smaller units (e.g., break a number sequence into small units - 132563 into 13, 25, 63).

27. Stop at various points during the presentation of information to check the student's comprehension.

28. Use concrete examples and experiences in sharing information with the student.

29. Have the student memorize the first sentence or line of a poem or song. Progressively have the student memorize the remainder as he/she experiences success.

30. Assess the meaningfulness of the material to the student. Remembering is more likely to occur when the material is meaningful and the student can relate to real experiences.

31. Have the student listen and take notes for the "Who, What, Where, When, How, and Why" while concepts are presented. (See Appendix for Outline Form.)

32. Present concepts following the outline of: (1) Who, (2) What, (3) Where, (4) When, (5) How, and (6) Why.

33. Have the student prepare for tests using the "Who, What, Where, When, How, and Why" system. (See Appendix for Outline Form.)

34. Develop tests and quizzes for the student using the "Who, What, Where, When, How, and Why" approach.

25 Fails to generalize knowledge from one situation to another

1. As soon as the student learns a skill, make certain that he/she applies it to a real-life situation (e.g., when the student learns to count by fives, have him/her practice adding nickels; when the student learns to tell the time through instructional materials, call upon him/her to tell time throughout the day; when the student learns to identify sight words in isolation, have him/her point out these words in context; when the student learns new spelling words, have him/her write a story using the words).

2. Make certain the student understands that all objects, people, ideas, actions, etc., can be grouped based on how they are alike. Provide the student with concrete examples (e.g., dogs, cats, cows, and horses are all mammals).

3. Give the student pairs of objects and ask him/her to name the ways in which they are alike and the ways they are different. Proceed from simple things which can be seen and touched to more abstract ideas which cannot be seen or touched.

4. Name a category or group and ask the student to identify as many things as possible which belong in the group. Begin with large categories (e.g., living things) and move to more specific categories (e.g., things which are green).

5. Ask the student to help make lists of some categories which fit inside larger categories (e.g., flowers, trees, and bushes are all categories which can be included in the plant category).

6. Identity related concepts and explain to the student how one can generalize to another (e.g., numbers to money, fuel to energy, words to sentences, etc.).

7. Have the student play analogy games involving multiple-choice possibilities (e.g., Food is to a person as gasoline is to a ____ (skateboard, automobile, house).).

8. Teach the student to look for shapes in the environment when teaching shapes (e.g., find all the circles in the room).

9. Deliver instructions by using examples of relationships (e.g., rely on what has already been learned, use examples from the student's environment, etc.).

10. Be certain to relate what the student has learned in one setting or situation to other situations (e.g., vocabulary words learned should be pointed out in reading selections, math word problems, story writing, etc.).

11. Call attention to situations in the classroom which generalize to more global situations (e.g., being on time for class is the same as being on time for work; school work not done during work time has to be made up before school, after school, or during recreational time, just as responsibilities at places of employment would have to be completed at night or weekends if not completed on the job; etc.).

12. Have the student write letters, fill out job applications, etc., in order to see the generalization of handwriting, spelling, grammar, sentence structure, etc., to real-life situations.

13. Provide the student with situations in which he/she can generalize skills learned in mathematics to a simulation of the use of money (e.g., making change, financing a car, computing interest earned from savings, etc.).

14. Make certain that the student is provided with an explanation of "why" he/she is learning particular information or skills (e.g., we learn to spell, read, and write in order to be able to communicate; we learn to solve math problems in order to be able to make purchases, use a checking account, measure, and cook; etc.).

15. Have the student develop a series of responses representing his/her ability to generalize from common situations in the environment (e.g., "We should drive no more than 55 miles per hour on our highways because . . ." Appropriate responses concern safety, conservation of fuel, care of vehicle, and fines for speeding.).

16. Use a variety of instructional approaches to help the student generalize knowledge gained to real-life situations (e.g., after studying the judicial system, provide a simulated courtroom trial; etc.).

17. Have the student listen and take notes for the ''Who, What, Where, When, How, and Why'' while concepts are presented. (See Appendix for Outline Form.)

18. Present concepts following the outline of: (1) Who, (2) What, (3) Where, (4) When, (5) How, and (6) Why.

19. Have the student prepare for tests using the ''Who, What, Where, When, How, and Why'' system. (See Appendix for Outline Form.)

20. Develop tests and quizzes for the student using the ''Who, What, Where, When, How, and Why'' approach.

1. Have the student take notes relative to important information he/she should remember.

2. Have the student tape record important information he/she should remember.

3. If the student has difficulty remembering information in written form, and if the student has difficulty remembering information he/she sees, present the information auditorily.

4. Have the student repeat/paraphrase important information he/she should remember.

5. Have the student outline, highlight, underline, or summarize information he/she should remember.

6. Use concrete examples and experiences in sharing information with the student.

7. Teach the student to recognize main points, important facts, etc.

8. Make certain the student has adequate opportunities for repetition of information through different experiences in order to enhance his/her memory.

9. Make certain information is presented to the student in the most clear and concise manner possible.

10. Reduce distracting stimuli when the student is attempting to remember important information.

11. Teach the student to rely on resources in the environment to recall information (e.g., notes, textbooks, pictures, etc.).

12. When the student is required to recall information, provide him/her with auditory cues to help him/her remember the information (e.g., key words, a brief oral description to clue the student, etc.).

13. Relate the information being presented to the student's previous experiences.

14. When the student is required to recall information, remind him/her of the situation in which the material was originally presented (e.g., key words, a brief oral description to clue the student, etc.).

15. Assess the meaningfulness of the material to the student. Remembering is more likely to occur when the material is meaningful and the student can relate to real experiences.

16. Have the student make notes, lists, etc., of things he/she needs to remember. The student carries these reminders with him/her.

17. Have the student follow a regular routine of daily events to establish consistency in his/her behavior pattern.

18. Teach the student to use mnemonic devices to recall information (e.g., to spell *geography*: George Ellen's Old Grandmother Rode A Pony Home Yesterday.).

19. Teach the student study techniques, such as SQ3R, to recall information.

20. Provide the student with verbal cues to stimulate recall of material.

21. Provide the student with a multi-sensory approach while learning new material in order to increase the likelihood that learning through several modalities will result in improved retention and recall.

22. Use techniques such as semantic mapping, color-coding and highlighting to stress important concepts to be recalled.

23. Have the student practice verbal repetition of information learned in order to increase accurate memory skills (e.g., phone numbers, dates of events, etc.).

24. Teach the student to use associative clues or mnemonic devices to remember information.

25. Provide the student with multiple opportunities to practice or use information immediately after it has been learned in order to increase retention of the information.

26. Have the student act as a peer tutor to another student in order to cement mastering of information learned and to prevent forgetting.

27. Have the student outline, highlight, underline or summarize information he/she should remember.

28. Review new information periodically during the week.

29. Teach the student how to organize information into smaller units (e.g., break a number sequence into smaller units - 132563 into 13, 25, 63).

30. Have the student listen and take notes for the "Who, What, Where, When, How, and Why" while concepts are presented. (See Appendix for Outline Form.)

31. Present concepts following the outline of: (1) Who, (2) What, (3) Where, (4) When, (5) How, and (6) Why.

32. Have the student prepare for tests using the "Who, What, Where, When, How, and Why" system. (See Appendix for Outline Form.)

27 Requires slow, sequential, substantially broken-down presentation of concepts

1. Evaluate the level of difficulty of the information to which the student is expected to listen (e.g., information communicated on the student's ability level).

2. Have the student question any directions, explanations, instructions he/she does not understand.

3. Have the student repeat or paraphrase what is said to him/her to determine what was heard.

4. Give the student short directions, explanations, or presentations of concepts. Gradually increase the length of the directions, explanations, or presentations of concepts as the student demonstrates success.

5. Maintain consistency in the delivery of verbal instructions.

6. Make certain the student is attending to the source of information (e.g., making eye contact, hands free of writing materials, looking at the assignment, etc.).

7. Provide the student with written directions and instructions to supplement verbal directions and instructions.

8. Emphasize or repeat word endings, key words, etc.

9. Speak clearly and concisely when delivering directions, explanations, and instructions.

10. Place the student near the source of information.

11. Reduce distracting stimuli (e.g., noise and motion in the classroom) in order to enhance the student's ability to listen successfully.

12. Stop at key points when delivering directions, explanations, and instructions in order to determine student comprehension.

13. Deliver directions, explanations, and instructions at an appropriate pace for the student.

14. Identify a list of word endings, key words, etc., that the student will practice listening for when someone is speaking.

15. Deliver oral questions and directions that involve only one concept or step. Gradually increase the number of concepts or steps as the student demonstrates success.

16. Move the student away from other students who may interfere with his/her ability to attend to directions, explanations, and instructions.

17. Teach the student listening skills (e.g., listen carefully, write down important points, ask for clarification, wait until all directions are received before beginning, etc.).

18. Use demonstrations along with the presentation of information.

19. Scan all materials for new words. Use simple terms when possible. Teach new vocabulary and provide practice through application.

20. Reduce abstractions by giving concrete examples and firsthand experiences.

21. Refer to previously presented, related information when presenting a new concept.

22. Prepare or obtain simplified manuals with definitions of technical vocabulary, simple vocabulary and sentence structure, step-by-step instructions, and diagrams or pictures.

23. Begin with concepts that are known and then sequence with skills or concepts not already mastered or integrated. Relationships will be more obvious when progressing to new skills and concepts.

24. Highlight or underline the important facts in reading material.

25. Rewrite instructions at an appropriate reading level for the student.

26. Identify the student's most efficient learning mode and use it consistently for the presentation of concepts.

27. If the student has difficulty with the oral presentation of concepts, provide the student with a written copy of material covered.

28. If the student has difficulty with the written presentation of concepts, provide the student with an oral presentation of material.

29. Tape record the presentation of concepts to be learned in order that the student can listen to it as often as necessary.

30. Have a peer repeat the presentation of concepts when the student does not understand.

31. When the student masters small units of information, have the student act as a peer tutor to teach units of information to another student.

32. Provide the student with the information he/she needs to learn in the most direct manner possible (e.g., list of facts, a summary of important points, outline of important events, etc.).

33. Have the student listen and take notes for "Who, What, Where, When, How, and Why" while concepts are presented. (See Appendix for Outline Form.)

34. Have the student use semantic mapping techniques when taking notes from the presentation of concepts. (See Appendix for Mapping Form.)

35. Present concepts following the outline of: (1) Who, (2) What, (3) Where, (4) When, (5) How, and (6) Why.

36. Develop tests and quizzes for the student using the "Who, What, Where, When, How, and Why" approach.

28 Turns in incomplete or inaccurately finished assignments

1. Speak with the student to explain: (a) what he/she is doing wrong (e.g., turning in work which is incomplete), and (b) what he/she should be doing (e.g., taking time to check for completeness of assignments).

2. Assess the appropriateness of the assignment for the student.

3. Provide the student with structure for all academic activities (e.g., specific directions, routine format for tasks, time units, etc.).

4. Interact frequently with the student to monitor his/her task performance.

5. Have the student question any directions, explanations, instructions he/she does not understand.

6. Assign a peer to accompany the student to specified activities in order to make certain the student has the necessary materials.

7. Provide the student with a list of necessary materials for each activity of the day.

8. Provide the student with verbal reminders of materials required for each activity.

9. Make certain that all educators who work with the student maintain consistent expectations of assignment completion.

10. Provide the student with assignment "forms" to enhance the completeness of assignments (e.g., provide blank number equations for word problems which the student fills in, etc.).

11. Provide the student with an organizational system for approaching assignments (e.g., name on paper, numbers listed on left column, etc.).

12. Provide the student with evaluative feedback for assignments completed (i.e., identify what the student did successfully, what errors were made, and what should be done to correct the errors).

13. Minimize the steps needed in order to complete the assignments accurately.

14. Maintain consistency in assignment format and expectations so as not to confuse the student.

15. It is not necessary to grade every assignment performed by the student. Assignments may be used to evaluate student ability or knowledge and provide feedback. Grades may not need to be assigned until mastery/minimal accuracy has been attained.

16. Have the student respond to tasks orally.

17. Have the student perform assignments, in which he/she might experience difficulty, in the resource room where the resource teacher can answer questions.

18. Provide the student with opportunities for review prior to grading assignments.

19. Arrange a time for the student to study with a peer tutor before completing a graded assignment.

20. Evaluate the appropriateness of the task to determine: (a) if the task is too difficult, and (b) if the length of time scheduled to complete the task is appropriate.

21. Assign a peer to work with the student in order to provide an acceptable model for the student to imitate.

22. Assign the student shorter tasks while increasing quality expectations.

23. Provide the student with clearly stated criteria for acceptable work.

24. Work the first few problems of an assignment with the student in order to make certain that he/she knows what to do, how to perform the assignment, etc.

25. Modify academic tasks (e.g., format, requirements, length, etc.).

26. Provide the student with clearly stated step-by-step directions for homework in order that someone at home may be able to provide assistance.

27. Make certain that homework assignments relate to concepts already taught rather than introducing a new concept.

28. Work through the steps of written directions as they are delivered in order to make certain the student follows the directions accurately.

29. Identify a peer to act as a model for the student to imitate turning in complete homework assignment.

30. Meet with parents to instruct them in appropriate ways to help the student with homework.

31. Identify a peer to act as a model for the student to imitate the appropriate following of written directions.

32. Teach the student the skills of following written directions: (e.g., read carefully, write down important points, ask for clarification, wait until all directions are received before beginning, etc.).

33. Give directions in a variety of ways to increase the probability of understanding (e.g., if the student fails to understand written directions, present them in verbal form).

34. Assign a peer to help the student with assignments.

35. Allow the student additional time to turn in assignments.

36. Repeat directions in order to increase the student's probability of understanding.

37. Provide the student with written directions for doing assignments.

38. Maintain consistency of expectations while keeping the expectations within the ability level of the student.

39. Maintain consistency in assigning homework (i.e., assign the same amount of homework each day).

40. Teach the student to prioritize assignments (e.g., according to importance, length, etc.).

41. Provide adequate time for completion of activities.

42. Establish a level of minimum accuracy which will be accepted as a level of mastery.

43. Deliver reinforcement for any and all measures of improvement.

44. Mastery should not be expected too soon after introducing new information, skills, etc.

45. Provide the student with self-checking materials, requiring correction before turning in assignments.

46. Should the student consistently fail to complete assignments with minimal accuracy, evaluate the appropriateness of tasks assigned.

47. If the student has difficulty completing homework assignments with minimal accuracy, provide a time during the day when he/she can receive assistance at school.

48. Make certain the assignments measure knowledge of content and not related skills such as reading or writing.

49. Have assignments read to the student.

50. Have the student read/review his/her schoolwork with the teacher in order that the student can become more aware of the quality of his/her work.

51. Provide the student with samples of work which may serve as models for acceptable quality (e.g., the student is to match the quality of the sample before turning in the assignment).

52. Provide the student with additional time to perform schoolwork in order to achieve quality.

53. Teach the student procedures for doing quality work (e.g., listen to directions, make certain directions are understood, work at an acceptable pace, check for errors, correct for neatness, copy the work over, etc.).

54. Recognize quality (e.g., display student's work, congratulate the student, etc.).

55. Conduct a preliminary evaluation of the work, requiring the student to make necessary corrections before final grading.

56. Provide the student with quality materials to perform the assignment (e.g., pencil with eraser, paper, dictionary, handwriting sample, etc.).

57. Provide the student with shorter assignments given more frequently. Increase the length of the assignments as the student demonstrates success.

58. Structure the environment in such a way as to provide the student with increased opportunity for help or assistance on academic or homework tasks (e.g., peer tutors, seat the student near the teacher or aide, etc.).

59. Provide the student with clearly stated written directions for homework in order that someone at home may be able to provide assistance.

29 Has difficulty taking class notes

1. Evaluate the appropriateness of note taking to determine: (a) if the task is too difficult, and (b) if the length of time scheduled to complete the task is appropriate.

2. Teach the student note-taking skills (e.g., copy main ideas from the board, identify main ideas from lectures, condense statements into a few key words, etc.).

3. Provide a standard format for note taking of directions and explanations (e.g., have paper and pencil or pen ready, listen for the steps in directions or explanations, write a shortened form of directions or explanations, ask to have any steps repeated when necessary, etc.).

4. Identify a peer to act as a model for the student to imitate appropriate note taking during class when necessary.

5. Have the student question any directions, explanations, instructions he/she does not understand.

6. Establish classroom rules (e.g., take notes when necessary, work on task, work quietly, remain in your seat, finish task, meet task expectations). Reiterate rules often and reinforce students for following rules.

7. Reinforce the student for taking notes during class when necessary based on the length of time he/she can be successful. Gradually increase the length of time required for reinforcement as the student demonstrates success.

8. Write a contract with the student specifying what behavior is expected (e.g., taking notes) and what reinforcement will be made available when the terms of the contract have been met.

9. Provide a standard format for note taking of lectures (e.g., have paper and pencil or pen ready, listen for main ideas of important information, write a shortened form of main ideas or important information, ask to have any main ideas or important information repeated when necessary, etc.).

10. While delivering instructions, directions, lectures, etc., point out to the student that information should be written in the form of notes.

11. Have the student practice legible manuscript or cursive handwriting during simulated and actual note-taking activities.

12. Have the student keep his/her notes organized in a folder for each subject or activity.

13. Check the student's notes before he/she begins an assignment in order to determine if they are correct and adequate for the assignment.

14. Provide the student with an outline or questions to be completed during teacher delivery of instructions, directions, lectures, etc.

15. Provide the student with samples of notes taken from actual instructions, directions, lectures, etc., given in the classroom in order that he/she may learn what information is necessary for note taking.

16. Make certain the student is in the best location in the classroom to receive information for note taking (e.g., near the board, teacher, or other source of information).

17. Make certain you can easily provide supervision of the student's note taking.

18. Make certain to maintain visibility to and from the student when delivering instructions, directions, lectures, etc., in order to enhance the likelihood of successful note taking.

19. Make certain that the instructions, directions, lectures, etc., are presented clearly and loudly enough for the student to hear.

20. Match the rate of delivery of instructions, directions, lectures, etc., to the student's ability to take notes.

21. Provide the student with both verbal and written instructions.

22. Provide instructions, directions, lectures, etc., in sequential steps in order to enhance student note taking.

23. Provide delivery of information in short segments for the student to take notes. Gradually increase the length of delivery as the student experiences success in note taking.

24. Make certain that the vocabulary used in delivering instructions, directions, lectures, etc., is appropriate for the student's ability level.

25. Place the student next to a peer in order that the student can copy notes taken by the peer.

26. Make certain the student has all necessary materials for note taking (e.g., paper, pencil, pen, etc.).

27. Make certain the student uses any necessary aids in order to facilitate note taking (e.g., eyeglasses, hearing aid, etc.).

28. Make certain the student has adequate surface space on which to write when taking notes (e.g., uncluttered desk top).

29. Reduce distracting stimuli that would interfere with the student's note taking (e.g., other students talking, outdoor activities, movement in the classroom, hallway noise, etc.).

30. Present the information in the most interesting manner possible.

31. Summarize the main points of instructions, directions, concepts, etc., for the student.

32. Identify the most successful note-taking style for the student. Encourage use of this approach for all note-taking activities. This will be more successful if all teachers the student comes in contact with allow this identified approach.

33. Provide the student with a limited outline of notes, and have the student add to the outline during class lecture.

34. Have the student listen and take notes for the "Who, What, Where, When, How, and Why" while concepts are presented. (See Appendix for Outline Form.)

35. Present concepts following the outline of: (1) Who, (2) What, (3) Where, (4) When, (5) How, and (6) Why.

36. Have the student prepare for tests using the "Who, What, Where, When, How, and Why" system. (See Appendix for Outline Form.)

30 Performs assignments carelessly

1. Provide the student with clearly stated criteria for acceptable work.

2. Speak with the student to explain: (a) what he/she is doing wrong (e.g., turning in work that is illegible, messy, etc.), and (b) what he/she should be doing (e.g., taking time to complete assignments with care, taking time to proofread).

3. Write a contract with the student specifying what behavior is expected (e.g., improving the quality of work) and what reinforcement will be made available when the terms of the contract have been met.

4. Communicate with parents (e.g., notes home, phone calls, etc.) in order to share information concerning the student's progress and so that they may reinforce the student at home for improving the quality of his/her work at school.

5. Evaluate the appropriateness of the task to determine: (a) if the task is too difficult, and (b) if the length of time scheduled to complete the task is appropriate.

6. Assign a peer to work with the student in order to provide an acceptable model for the student to imitate.

7. Allow the student to perform schoolwork in a quiet place (e.g., study carrel, library, resource room, etc.) in order to reduce distractions.

8. Assign the student shorter tasks while increasing quality expectations.

9. Supervise the student while he/she is performing schoolwork in order to monitor quality.

10. Have the student read/review schoolwork with the teacher in order that the student can become more aware of the quality of his/her work.

11. Provide the student with samples of work which may serve as models for acceptable quality (e.g., the student is to match the quality of the sample before turning in the assignment).

12. Provide the student additional time to perform schoolwork in order to achieve quality.

13. Teach the student procedures for doing quality work (e.g., listen to directions, make certain directions are understood, work at an acceptable pace, check for errors, correct for neatness, copy the work over, etc.).

14. Recognize quality (e.g., display student's work, congratulate the student, etc.).

15. Conduct a preliminary evaluation of the work, requiring the student to make necessary corrections before final grading.

16. Provide the student with quality materials to perform the assignment (e.g., pencil with eraser, paper, dictionary, handwriting sample, etc.).

17. Make certain that all educators who work with the student maintain consistent expectations of quality of work.

1. Reinforce the student for attempting a new assignment/task: (a) give the student a tangible reward (e.g., classroom privileges, line leading, passing out materials, five minutes free time, etc.) when he/she attempts a new assignment/task, or (b) give the student an intangible reward (e.g., praise, handshake, smile, etc.) when he/she attempts a new assignment/task.

2. Speak with the student to explain: (a) what he/she is doing wrong (e.g., not attempting a new task), and (b) what he/she should be doing (e.g., asking for assistance or clarification, following directions, starting on time, etc.).

3. Reinforce those students in the classroom who attempt a new assignment/task.

4. Reinforce the student for attempting a new assignment/task within the length of time he/she can be successful. Gradually decrease the amount of time to begin the task in order to be reinforced as the student demonstrates success.

5. Write a contract with the student specifying what behavior is expected (e.g., attempting a new assignment/task) and what reinforcement will be made available when the terms of the contract have been met.

6. Communicate with parents (e.g., notes home, phone calls, etc.) in order to share information concerning the student's progress and so that they may reinforce the student at home for attempting a new assignment/task at school.

7. Evaluate the appropriateness of the task to determine: (a) if the task is too difficult, and (b) if the length of time scheduled to complete the task is appropriate.

8. Have the student question any directions, explanations, and instructions he/she does not understand.

9. Reduce distracting stimuli (e.g., place the student on the front row, provide a carrel or ''office'' space away from distractions, etc.). This is used as a means of reducing distracting stimuli and not as a form of punishment.

10. Assign a peer or volunteer to help the student begin a task.

11. Structure the environment in such a way as to provide the student with increased opportunity for help or assistance.

12. Assess the quality and clarity of directions, explanations, and instructions given to the student.

13. Have the student maintain a record (e.g., chart or graph) of his/her performance in attempting new assignments/tasks.

14. Communicate clearly to the student when it is time to begin.

15. Have the student time his/her activities in order to monitor his/her own behavior and accept time limits.

16. Present the task in the most interesting and attractive manner possible.

17. Maintain mobility in order to provide assistance to the student.

18. Structure time units in order that the student knows exactly how long he/she has to work and when he/she must be finished.

19. Provide the student with more than enough time to finish an activity and decrease the amount of time as the student demonstrates success.

20. Give directions in a variety of ways in order to increase the probability of understanding (e.g., if the student fails to understand verbal directions, present them in written form).

21. Have the student repeat the directions orally to the teacher.

22. Give a signal (e.g., clapping hands, turning lights off and on, etc.) before giving verbal directions.

23. Provide the student with a predetermined signal when he/she is not beginning a task (e.g., verbal cue, hand signal, etc.).

24. Tell the student that directions will only be given once.

25. Rewrite directions at a lower reading level.

26. Deliver verbal directions in a more basic way.

27. Help the student with the first few items on a task and gradually reduce the amount of help over time.

28. Follow a less desirable task with a highly desirable task making the completion of the first necessary to perform the second.

29. Provide the student with a Schedule of Daily Events in order that he/she knows exactly what and how much there is to do in a day. (See Appendix.)

30. Prevent the student from becoming over-stimulated by an activity (e.g., frustrated, angry, etc.) by modifying assignments.

31. Specify exactly what is to be done for the completion of a task (e.g., make definite starting and stopping points, a minimum requirement, etc.).

32. Require the student to begin each assignment within a specified period of time (e.g., three minutes, five minutes, etc.).

33. Provide the student with shorter tasks given more frequently.

34. Provide the student with a selection of assignments, requiring him/her to choose a minimum number from the total (e.g., present the student with ten academic tasks from which he/she must finish six that day).

35. Start with a single problem and add more problems to the task over time.

36. Provide the student with a choice of problems to do on the assignment, requiring him/her to choose a minimum number from the total (e.g., present the student with ten math problems from which he/she must complete seven).

37. Reduce the emphasis on competition (e.g., academic or social). Fear of failure may cause the student to refuse to attempt new assignments/tasks.

38. Provide the student with self-checking materials in order that he/she may check work privately, thus reducing the fear of public failure.

39. Have the student attempt a new assignment/task in a private place (e.g., carrel, "office," quiet study area, etc.) in order to reduce the fear of public failure.

40. Have the student practice a new skill (e.g., jumping rope, dribbling a basketball, etc.) alone, with a peer, or with the teacher before the entire group attempts the activity.

41. Provide the student with the opportunity to perform the assignment/task in a variety of ways (e.g., on tape, with a calculator, orally, etc.).

42. Allow the student to perform new assignments/tasks in a variety of places in the building (e.g., resource room, library, learning center, etc.).

43. Provide the student with a sample of the assignment/task which has been partially completed by a peer or teacher (e.g., book report, project, etc.).

44. Do not require the student to complete the assignment/task in one sitting.

45. Allow the student the option of performing the assignment/task at another time (e.g., earlier in the day, later, on another day, etc.).

46. Explain to the student that work not done during work time will have to be made up at other times (e.g., during recess, before school, after school, during lunch time, etc.).

47. Make certain that the student has all the materials he/she needs in order to perform the assignment/task.

48. Have the student explain to the teacher what he/she thinks he/she should do in order to perform the assignment/task.

49. Deliver directions/instructions before handing out materials.

50. Provide the student with optional courses of action to prevent total refusal to obey teacher directives.

51. Teach the student direction-following skills: (a) listen carefully, (b) ask questions, (c) use environmental cues, (d) rely on examples provided, and (e) wait until directions are given before beginning.

52. Present directions following the outline of: (1) What, (2) How, (3) Materials, and (4) When. (See Appendix for Assignment Form.)

53. Have the student take notes when directions are being given following the "What, How, Materials, and When" format. (See Appendix for Assignment Form.)

32 Does not perform or complete classroom assignments during class time

1. Reinforce the student for attempting and completing class assignments: (a) give the student a tangible reward (e.g., classroom privileges, line leading, passing out materials, five minutes free time, etc.) when he/she attempts and completes class assignments, or (b) give the student an intangible reward (e.g., praise, handshake, smile, etc.) for attempting and completing class assignments.

2. Speak with the student to explain: (a) what he/she is doing wrong (e.g., not completing assignments) and (b) what he/she should be doing (e.g., completing assignments during class).

3. Establish classroom rules (e.g., work on task, work quietly, remain in your seat, finish task, meet task requirements). Reiterate rules often and reinforce students for following rules.

4. Reinforce those students in the classroom who attempt and complete assignments during class time.

5. Reinforce the student for attempting and completing assignments based on the amount of work he/she successfully completes. Gradually increase the amount of work required for reinforcement as the student demonstrates success.

6. Write a contract with the student specifying what behavior is expected (e.g., attempting and completing class assignments) and what reinforcement will be made available when the terms of the contract have been met.

7. Have the student keep a chart or graph representing the number of class assignments completed.

8. Evaluate the appropriateness of the task to determine: (a) if the task is too difficult, and (b) if the length of time scheduled for the task is appropriate.

9. Assign a peer to help the student with class assignments.

10. Assess the degree of task difficulty in comparison with the student's ability to perform the task.

11. Assign the student shorter tasks (e.g., modify a 20-problem math activity to 4 activities of 5 problems each, to be done at various times during the day). Gradually increase the number of problems over time.

12. Present tasks in the most attractive and interesting manner possible.

13. Reduce distracting stimuli (e.g., place the student in the front row, provide a carrel or quiet place away from distractions, etc.). This is used as a means of reducing stimuli and not as a form of punishment.

14. Interact frequently with the student in order to maintain involvement with class assignments (e.g., ask the student questions, ask the student's opinions, stand close to the student, seat the student near the teacher's desk, etc.).

15. Allow the student additional time to complete class assignments.

16. Supervise the student during class assignments in order to maintain on-task behavior.

17. Deliver directions orally in order to increase the probability of the student's understanding of class assignments.

18. Repeat directions in order to increase the probability of understanding.

19. Encourage the student to ask for clarification of directions for classroom assignments.

20. Follow a less desirable task with a highly desirable task, making the completion of the first necessary to perform the second.

21. Give directions in a variety of ways to increase the probability of understanding (e.g., if the student fails to understand verbal directions, present them in written form).

22. Provide the student with step-by-step written directions for doing class assignments.

23. Make certain the student understands the natural consequences of failing to complete assignments (e.g., students who do not finish their work will not get to do more desirable activities).

24. Allow the student to perform alternative assignments. Gradually introduce more components of the regular assignments until those assignments are routinely performed.

25. Explain to the student that work not done during work time will have to be done during other times (e.g., break time, recreational time, after school, etc.).

26. Take steps to deal with student refusal to perform an assignment in order that the rest of the group will not be exposed to contagion (e.g., refrain from arguing with the student, place the student in a carrel or other quiet place to work, remove the student from the group or classroom, etc.).

27. Maintain consistency of expectations while keeping expectations within the ability level of the student.

28. Allow the student the option of performing the assignment at another time (e.g., earlier in the day, later, on another day, or take the assignment home).

29. Provide the student with a selection of assignments and require him/her to choose a minimum number from the total amount (e.g., present the student with ten academic tasks from which he/she must finish six that day).

30. Maintain consistency in daily routine.

31. Work a few problems with the student on an assignment in order to serve as a model and help the student begin a task.

32. Reinforce the student for beginning, staying on, and completing assignments.

33. Communicate with parents (e.g., notes home, phone calls, etc.) in order to share information concerning the student's progress and so that they may reinforce the student at home for completing assignments at school.

34. Identify a peer to act as a model for the student to imitate appropriate completion of assignments.

35. Have the student question any directions, explanations, instructions he/she does not understand.

36. Assess the quality and clarity of directions, explanations, and instructions given to the student.

37. Structure the environment in such a way as to provide the student with increased opportunity for help or assistance.

38. Communicate clearly to the student the length of time he/she has to complete the assignment.

39. Communicate clearly to the student when the assignment should be completed.

40. Have the student time his/her assignments in order to monitor his/her own behavior and accept time limits.

41. Structure time units in order that the student knows exactly how long he/she has to work and when he/she must be finished.

42. Provide the student with more than enough time to finish an activity and decrease the amount of time as the student demonstrates success.

43. Have the student repeat the directions orally to the teacher.

44. Rewrite directions at a lower reading level.

45. Practice direction-following skills on nonacademic tasks.

46. Provide the student with a Schedule of Daily Events in order that he/she knows exactly what and how much there is to do in a day. (See Appendix.)

47. Prevent the student from becoming over-stimulated by an activity (e.g., frustrated, angry, etc.) by modifying assignments.

48. Specify exactly what is to be done for the completion of the task (e.g., indicate definite starting and stopping points, indicate a minimum requirement, etc.).

49. Require the student to begin each assignment within a specified period of time (e.g., three minutes, five minutes, etc.).

50. Provide the student with shorter tasks given more frequently.

51. Provide clearly stated directions in written or verbal form (e.g., make the directions as simple and concrete as possible).

52. Interact frequently with the student in order to help him/her follow directions for the assignment.

53. Provide alternatives for the traditional format of directions (e.g., tape record directions, summarize directions, directions given by peers, etc.).

54. Reduce directions to steps (e.g., give the student each additional step after completion of the previous step).

55. Make certain the student achieves success when following directions.

56. Reduce the emphasis on early completion. Hurrying to complete assignments may cause the student to fail to follow directions.

57. Allow the student access to pencils, pens, etc., only after directions have been given.

58. Establish assignment rules (e.g., listen to directions, wait until all directions have been given, ask questions about anything you do not understand, begin assignments only when you are certain about what you are supposed to do, make certain you have all necessary materials, etc.).

59. Make certain that the student is attending to the teacher when directions are given (e.g., making eye contact, hands free of writing materials, looking at assignment, etc.).

60. Maintain visibility to and from the student in order to make certain the student is attending. The teacher should be able to see the student and the student should be able to see the teacher, making eye contact possible at all times.

61. Along with the student, chart those assignments that have been completed in a given period of time.

62. Present one assignment at a time. As each assignment is completed, deliver reinforcement along with the presentation of the next assignment.

63. Have the student use a timer in order to complete tasks within a given period of time.

64. Reduce emphasis on academic and social competition. Fear of failure may cause the student to not want to complete the required number of assignments in a given period of time.

65. Have the student complete his/her assignments in a private place (e.g., carrel, "office," quiet study area, etc.) in order to reduce the anxiety of public failure.

66. Provide the student with the opportunity to perform assignments/activities in a variety of ways (e.g., on tape, with a calculator, orally, etc.).

67. Have the student explain to the teacher what he/she should do in order to perform the assignment.

33 Does not turn in homework assignments

1. Reinforce the student for turning in homework assignments: (a) give the student a tangible reward (e.g., classroom privileges, line leading, passing out materials, five minutes free time, etc.) when he/she turns in a homework assignment, or (b) give the student an intangible reward (e.g., praise, handshake, smile, etc.) for turning in a homework assignment.

2. Speak to the student to explain: (a) what he/she is doing wrong (e.g., not turning in homework assignments), and (b) what he/she should be doing (e.g., completing homework assignments and returning them to school).

3. Establish homework assignment rules (e.g., work on task, finish task, meet task expectations, turn in task). Reiterate rules often and reinforce students for following rules.

4. Reinforce those students in the classroom who turn in their homework assignments.

5. Reinforce the student for turning in his/her homework. Gradually increase the number of times required for reinforcement as the student demonstrates success.

6. Write a contract with the student specifying what behavior is expected (e.g., turning in homework) and what reinforcement will be made available when the terms of the contract have been met.

7. Communicate with parents (e.g., notes home, phone calls, etc.) in order to share information concerning the student's progress and so that they may reinforce the student at home for turning in homework at school.

8. Evaluate the appropriateness of the homework assignment to determine: (a) if the task is too difficult, and (b) if the length of time scheduled to complete the task is appropriate.

9. Identify a peer to act as a model for the student to imitate turning in homework assignments.

10. Chart homework assignments completed.

11. Meet with parents to instruct them in appropriate ways to help the student with homework.

12. Have the student chart or graph the number of homework assignments he/she turns in to the teacher.

13. Have the student question any directions, explanations, instructions he/she does not understand.

14. Assess the appropriateness of assigning the student homework if his/her ability or circumstances at home make it impossible to complete and return the assignments.

15. Assign a peer to help the student with homework.

16. Present the tasks in the most attractive and interesting manner possible.

17. Allow the student additional time to turn in homework assignments.

18. Deliver directions orally in order to increase the probability of the student's understanding of homework assignments.

19. Repeat directions in order to increase the student's probability of understanding.

20. Allow the student to perform a highly desirable task when his/her homework has been turned in to the teacher.

21. Give directions in a variety of ways in order to increase the probability of understanding (e.g., if the student fails to understand verbal directions, present them in written form).

22. Provide the student with written directions for doing homework assignments.

23. Allow the student to perform alternative homework assignments. Gradually introduce more components of the regular homework assignments until those assignments are routinely performed and returned to school.

24. Allow natural consequences to occur for failure to turn in homework assignments (e.g., students who do not finish their homework do not get to engage in more desirable activities).

25. Introduce the student to other resource persons who may be of help in doing homework (e.g., other teachers, librarian, etc.).

26. Encourage the parents to provide the student with a quiet, comfortable place and adequate time to do homework.

27. Take proactive steps to deal with student refusal to perform a homework assignment in order that the rest of the group will not be exposed to contagion (e.g., refrain from arguing with the student, place the student at a carrel or other quiet place to work, remove the student from the group or classroom, etc.).

28. Maintain consistency of expectations and keep the expectations within the ability level of the student.

29. Work a few problems with the student on homework assignments in order to serve as a model and start the student on a task.

30. Make certain that homework is designed to provide drill activities rather than introduce new information.

31. Develop a contract with the student and his/her parents requiring that homework be done before more desirable activities take place at home (e.g., playing, watching television, going out for the evening, etc.).

32. In case the student should fail to take necessary materials home, provide a set of these materials to be kept at home, and send directions for homework with the student.

33. Assign small amounts of homework initially, gradually increasing the amount as the student demonstrates success (e.g., one or two problems to perform may be sufficient to begin the homework process).

34. Find a tutor (e.g., peer, volunteer, etc.) to work with the student at home.

35. Maintain consistency in assigning homework (i.e., assign the same amount of homework each day).

36. Provide time at school for homework completion when the student cannot be successful in performing assignments at home.

37. Provide the student with a book bag, backpack, etc., to take homework assignments and materials to and from home.

38. Send homework assignments and materials directly to the home with someone other than the student (e.g., brother or sister, neighbor, bus driver, etc.).

39. Schedule the student's time at school so that homework will not be necessary if he/she takes advantage of the time provided to complete assignments at school.

40. Reinforce those students who complete their assignments at school during the time provided.

41. Create a learning center at school, open the last hour of each school day, where professional educators are available to help with homework assignments.

42. Do not use homework as a punishment (i.e., homework should not be assigned as a consequence for inappropriate behavior at school).

34 Does not prepare for assigned activities

1. Reinforce the student for being prepared for assigned activities: (a) give the student a tangible reward (e.g., classroom privileges, line leading, passing out materials, five minutes free time, etc.) when he/she is prepared for assigned activities, or (b) give the student an intangible reward (e.g., praise, handshake, smile, etc.) for being prepared for assigned activities.

2. Speak to the student to explain: (a) what he/she is doing wrong (e.g., failing to study, complete assignments, bring materials to class, etc.) and (b) what he/she should be doing (e.g., studying, completing assignments, bringing materials to class, etc.).

3. Establish classroom rules (e.g., work on task, work quietly, remain in your seat, finish task, meet task expectations). Reiterate rules often and reinforce students for following rules.

4. Reinforce those students in the classroom who are prepared for assigned activities.

5. Reinforce the student for being prepared for assigned activities based on the number of times he/she can be successful. Gradually increase the number of times required for reinforcement as the student demonstrates success.

6. Write a contract with the student specifying what behavior is expected (e.g., studying for tests or quizzes) and what reinforcement will be made available when the terms of the contract have been met.

7. Communicate with parents (e.g., notes home, phone calls, etc.) in order to share information concerning the student's progress and so that they may reinforce the student at home for being prepared for assigned activities at school.

8. Evaluate the appropriateness of the task to determine: (a) if the task is too difficult, and (b) if the length of time scheduled to complete the task is appropriate.

9. Identify a peer to act as a model for the student to imitate being prepared for assigned activities.

10. Have the student question any directions, explanations, instructions he/she does not understand.

11. Assign a peer to accompany the student to specified activities in order to make certain the student has the necessary materials.

12. Provide the student with a list of necessary materials for each activity of the day.

13. Provide the student with verbal reminders of materials required for each activity.

14. Provide time at the beginning of each day/activity for the student to organize his/her materials (e.g., before school, recess, lunch, etc.).

15. Act as a model for being prepared for assigned activities.

16. At the end of the day, remind the student what materials are required for specified activities for the next day (e.g., send a note home, verbal reminder, etc.).

17. Have the student establish a routine to follow before coming to class (e.g., check which activity is next, determine what materials are necessary, collect materials, etc.).

18. Have the student leave necessary materials at specified activity areas.

19. Provide the student with a container in which to carry necessary materials for specified activities (e.g., back pack, book bag, briefcase, etc.).

20. Assess the quality and clarity of directions, explanations, and instructions given to the student.

21. Provide the student with structure for all academic activities (e.g., specific directions, routine format for tasks, time units, etc.).

22. Minimize materials needed.

23. Make certain that failure to be prepared for assigned activities results in loss of the opportunity to participate in activities or a failing grade for that day's activity.

24. Provide the student with adequate time at school to prepare for assigned activities (e.g., supervised study time).

25. Assign a peer tutor to work with the student in order to prepare him/her for assigned activities.

26. Reduce the number/length of assignments. Gradually increase the number/length of assignments as the student demonstrates success.

27. Specify exactly what is to be done for the completion of assignments (e.g., make definite starting and stopping points, determine a minimum requirement, etc.).

28. Allow natural consequences to occur when the student is unprepared for assigned activities (e.g., the student will fail a test or quiz, work not done during work time must be completed during recreational time, etc.).

29. Ask the student why he/she is unprepared for assigned activities. The student may have the most accurate perception.

30. Communicate with parents or guardians in order to inform them of the student's homework assignments and what they can do to help the student prepare for assigned activities.

31. Provide the student with written directions to follow in preparing for all assigned activities.

32. Have the student listen and take notes for the ''Who, What, Where, When, How and Why'' while concepts are presented. (See Appendix for Outline Form.)

33. Present concepts following the outline of: (1) Who, (2) What, (3) Where, (4) When, (5) How, (6) Why, and (7) Vocabulary.

34. Have the student prepare for tests using the ''Who, What, Where, When, How, and Why'' method. (See Appendix for Outline Form.)

35. Present directions following the outline of: (1) What, (2) How, (3) Materials, and (4) When. (See Appendix for Assignment Form.)

36. Have the student take notes when directions are being given following the ''What, How, Materials, and When'' format. (See Appendix for Assignment Form.)

37. Teach the student skills for taking tests. (See Appendix for Test-Taking Skills.)

38. Teach the student how to study for a test. (See Appendix for Studying for a Test.)

39. Teach the student the skills for taking notes. (See Appendix for Note Taking.)

40. Provide the student with a written list of assignments to be performed each day and have him/her check each assignment as it is completed.

41. Provide individual assistance to the student in order to help him/her prepare for assigned activities (e.g., time set aside during the day, during study hall, after school, etc.).

42. Identify other personnel in the school who may assist the student in preparing for assigned activities (e.g., aide, librarian, other teachers, etc.).

35 Does not remain on task

1. Reinforce the student for staying on task in the classroom: (a) give the student a tangible reward (e.g., classroom privileges, line leading, passing out materials, five minutes free time, etc.) when he/she stays on task, or (b) give the student an intangible reward (e.g., praise, handshake, smile, etc.) for staying on task.

2. Speak to the student to explain: (a) what he/she is doing wrong (e.g., failing to attend to tasks) and (b) what he/she should be doing (e.g., attending to tasks).

3. Establish classroom rules (e.g., work on task, work quietly, remain in your seat, finish task, meet task expectations). Reiterate rules often and reinforce students for following rules.

4. Reinforce those students in the classroom who demonstrate on-task behavior.

5. Reinforce the student for attending to tasks based on the length of time he/she can be successful. Gradually increase the length of time required for reinforcement as the student demonstrates success.

6. Write a contract with the student specifying what behavior is expected (e.g., establish a reasonable length of time to stay on task) and what reinforcement will be made available when the terms of the contract have been met.

7. Communicate with parents (e.g., notes home, phone calls, etc.) in order to share information concerning the student's progress and so that they may reinforce the student at home for staying on task in the classroom.

8. Identify a peer to act as a model for the student to imitate on-task behavior.

9. Have the student question any directions, explanations, instructions he/she does not understand.

10. Evaluate the auditory and visual stimuli in the classroom in order to determine the level of stimuli the student can respond to in an appropriate manner.

11. Reduce auditory and visual stimuli to a level at which the student can successfully function. Gradually allow auditory and visual stimuli to increase as the student demonstrates that he/she can successfully tolerate the increased levels.

12. Seat the student so that he/she experiences the least amount of auditory and visual stimuli.

13. Provide the student with a quiet place in which to work, where auditory and visual stimuli are reduced. This is used to reduce distracting stimuli and not as a form of punishment.

14. Seat the student away from those peers who create the most auditory and visual stimulation in the classroom.

15. Provide the student with a carrel or divider at his/her desk to reduce auditory and visual stimuli.

16. Make certain that all auditory and visual stimuli in the classroom are reduced as much as possible for all learners.

17. Provide the student with the opportunity to move to a quiet place in the classroom any time that auditory and visual stimuli interfere with his/her ability to function successfully.

18. Provide the student with earphones to wear if auditory stimuli interfere with his/her ability to function. Gradually remove the earphones as the student can more successfully function in the presence of auditory stimuli.

19. Allow the student to close the door or windows in order to reduce auditory and visual stimuli from outside of the classroom.

20. Require the student to be productive in the presence of auditory and visual stimuli for short periods of time. Gradually increase the length of time the student is required to be productive as he/she becomes successful.

21. Have the student work with a peer tutor in order to maintain attention to tasks.

22. Provide the student with shorter tasks which do not require extended attention in order to be successful. Gradually increase the length of the tasks as the student demonstrates success.

23. Have the student engage in small group activities (e.g., free time, math, reading, etc.) in order to reduce the level of auditory and visual stimuli in the group. Gradually increase group size as the student can function successfully.

24. Model for the student appropriate behavior in the presence of auditory and visual stimuli in the classroom (e.g., continuing to work, asking for quiet, moving to a quieter part of the classroom, etc.).

25. Remove the student from an activity until he/she can demonstrate appropriate on-task behavior.

26. Assign the student shorter tasks but more of them (e.g., modify a 20-problem math activity to 4 activities of 5 problems each, to be performed at various times during the day). Gradually increase the number of problems for each activity as the student demonstrates success.

27. Present tasks in the most attractive and interesting manner possible.

28. Assess the degree of task difficulty in relation to the student's ability to successfully perform the task.

29. Interact frequently with the student in order to maintain his/her involvement in the activity (e.g., ask the student questions, ask the student's opinion, stand close to the student, seat the student near the teacher's desk, etc.).

30. Provide the student with a timer which he/she may use to increase the amount of time during which he/she maintains attention (e.g., have the student work on the activity until the timer goes off).

31. Provide the student with a predetermined signal (e.g., hand signal, verbal cue, etc.) when he/she begins to display off-task behaviors.

32. Structure the environment to reduce the opportunity for off-task behavior. Reduce lag time by providing the student with enough activities to maintain productivity.

33. Make certain the student has all necessary materials to perform assignments.

34. Make certain the student knows what to do when he/she cannot successfully perform assignments (e.g., raise hand, ask for assistance, go to the teacher, etc.).

35. Maintain visibility to and from the student. The teacher should be able to see the student and the student should be able to see the teacher, making eye contact possible at all times.

36. Make certain to recognize the student when his/her hand is raised in order to convey that assistance will be provided as soon as possible.

37. Teach the student how to manage his/her time until the teacher can provide assistance (e.g., try the problem again, go on to the next problem, wait quietly, etc.).

36 Is easily distracted by visual and auditory stimuli in the classroom

1. Reinforce the student for staying on task in the classroom: (a) give the student a tangible reward (e.g., classroom privileges, line leading, passing out materials, five minutes free time, etc.) when he/she stays on task, or (b) give the student an intangible reward (e.g., praise, handshake, smile, etc.) for staying on task.

2. Speak to the student to explain: (a) what he/she is doing wrong (e.g., failing to attend to tasks), and (b) what he/she should be doing (e.g., attending to tasks).

3. Establish classroom rules (e.g., work on task, work quietly, remain in your seat, finish task, meet task expectations). Reiterate rules often and reinforce students for following rules.

4. Reinforce those students in the classroom who demonstrate on-task behavior.

5. Reinforce the student for attending to tasks based on the length of time he/she can be successful. Gradually increase the length of time required for reinforcement as the student demonstrates success.

6. Write a contract with the student specifying what behavior is expected (e.g., establish a reasonable length of time to stay on task) and what reinforcement will be made available when the terms of the contract have been met.

7. Communicate with parents (e.g., notes home, phone calls, etc.) in order to share information concerning the student's progress and so that they may reinforce the student at home for staying on task in the classroom.

8. Identify a peer to act as a model for the student to imitate on-task behavior.

9. Have the student question any directions, explanations, instructions he/she does not understand.

10. Seat the student so that he/she experiences the least amount of auditory and visual stimuli.

11. Evaluate the auditory and visual stimuli in the classroom in order to determine the level of stimuli to which the student can respond in an appropriate manner.

12. Reduce auditory and visual stimuli to a level at which the student can successfully function. Gradually allow auditory and visual stimuli to increase as the student demonstrates that he/she can successfully tolerate the increased levels.

13. Provide the student with a quiet place in which to work where auditory and visual stimuli are reduced. This is used to reduce distracting stimuli and not as a form of punishment.

14. Seat the student away from those peers who create the most auditory and visual stimulation in the classroom.

15. Provide the student with a carrel or divider at his/her desk to reduce auditory and visual stimuli.

16. Make certain that all auditory and visual stimuli in the classroom are reduced as much as possible for all learners.

17. Provide the student with the opportunity to move to a quiet place in the classroom any time that auditory and visual stimuli interfere with his/her ability to function successfully.

18. Provide the student with earphones to wear if auditory stimuli interfere with his/her ability to function. Gradually remove the earphones as the student can more successfully function in the presence of auditory stimuli.

19. Allow the student to close the door or windows in order to reduce auditory and visual stimuli from outside of the classroom.

20. Remove the student from an activity until he/she can demonstrate appropriate on-task behavior.

21. Require the student to be productive in the presence of auditory and visual stimuli for short periods of time. Gradually increase the length of time the student is required to be productive as he/she becomes successful.

22. Provide the student with shorter tasks which do not require extended attention in order to be successful. Gradually increase the length of the tasks as the student demonstrates success.

23. Have the student engage in small group activities (e.g., free time, math, reading, etc.) in order to reduce the level of auditory and visual stimuli in the group. Gradually increase group size as the student can function successfully.

24. Model for the student appropriate behavior in the presence of auditory and visual stimuli in the classroom (e.g., continuing to work, asking for quiet, moving to a quieter part of the classroom, etc.).

25. Assign the student shorter tasks but more of them (e.g., modify a 20-problem math activity to 4 activities of 5 problems each, to be performed at various times during the day). Gradually increase the number of problems for each activity as the student demonstrates success.

26. Present tasks in the most attractive and interesting manner possible.

27. Assess the degree of task difficulty in relation to the student's ability to successfully perform the task.

28. Interact frequently with the student in order to maintain his/her involvement in the activity (e.g., ask the student questions, ask the student's opinion, stand close to the student, seat the student near the teacher's desk, etc.).

29. Provide the student with a timer which he/she may use to increase the amount of time during which he/she maintains attention (e.g., have the student work on the activity until the timer goes off).

30. Provide the student with a predetermined signal (e.g., hand signal, verbal cue, etc.) when he/she begins to display off-task behaviors.

31. Structure the environment to reduce the opportunity for off-task behavior. Reduce lag time by providing the student with enough activities to maintain productivity.

32. Have the student work with a peer tutor in order to maintain attention to tasks.

33. Make certain the student has all necessary materials to perform assignments.

34. Make certain the student knows what to do when he/she cannot successfully perform assignments (e.g., raise hand, ask for assistance, go to the teacher, etc.).

35. Maintain visibility to and from the student. The teacher should be able to see the student and the student should be able to see the teacher, making eye contact possible at all times.

36. Make certain to recognize the student when his/her hand is raised, in order to convey that assistance will be provided as soon as possible.

37. Teach the student how to manage his/her time until the teacher can provide assistance (e.g., try the problem again, go on to the next problem, wait quietly, etc.).

37 Is unable to work appropriately with peers in a tutoring situation

1. Reinforce the student for working appropriately with peers in a tutoring situation: (a) give the student a tangible reward (e.g., classroom privileges, line leading, passing out materials, five minutes free time, etc.) when he/she works appropriately with peers in a tutoring situation, or (b) give the student an intangible reward (e.g., praise, handshake, smile, etc.) for working appropriately with peers in a tutoring situation.

2. Speak to the student to explain: (a) what he/she is doing wrong (e.g., not attending to the tutor, arguing with peers, etc.) and (b) what he/she should be doing (e.g., attending to the tutor, doing his/her own work, etc.).

3. Establish tutoring rules (e.g., work on task, work quietly, remain in your seat, finish task, meet task expectations). Reiterate rules often and reinforce students for following rules.

4. Reinforce those students in the classroom who work appropriately with peers in a tutoring situation.

5. Reinforce the student for working appropriately with peers in a tutoring situation based on the length of time he/she can be successful. Gradually increase the length of time required for reinforcement as the student demonstrates success.

6. Write a contract with the student specifying what behavior is expected (e.g., attending to the tutor, taking turns, sharing materials, etc.) and what reinforcement will be made available when the terms of the contract have been met.

7. Communicate with parents (e.g., notes home, phone calls, etc.) in order to share information concerning the student's progress and so that they may reinforce the student at home for working appropriately with peers in a tutoring situation at school.

8. Evaluate the appropriateness of the tutoring situation in order to determine: (a) if the task is too difficult, and (b) if the length of time scheduled to complete the task is appropriate.

9. Identify a peer to act as a model for the student to imitate working appropriately with peers in a tutoring situation.

10. Have the student question any directions, explanations, instructions he/she does not understand.

11. Make certain that the student and peer tutor are compatible (e.g., the student accepts his/her role in the tutoring situation, the student and peer tutor are accepting of one another, the peer tutor has skills and knowledge to share, etc.).

12. Be certain that the opportunity to work with a peer tutor is contingent upon appropriate behavior prior to and during the tutoring situation.

13. Teach the student appropriate behavior for peer tutoring situations (e.g., follow directions, work quietly, take turns, share materials, etc.).

14. Supervise tutoring situations closely in order to make certain that the student's behavior is appropriate, the task is appropriate, he/she is learning from the situation, etc.

15. Make certain the tutoring activity involves practice, drill, or repetition of information or skills previously presented.

16. Determine which peer(s) the student would most prefer to interact with in tutoring situations and attempt to group these students together for peer tutoring.

17. Assign an outgoing, nonthreatening peer to act as a peer tutor.

18. Structure the environment so that the student has many opportunities for success in the tutoring situation.

19. Assign the student to tutoring situations in which he/she is likely to interact successfully with other peers being tutored.

20. Conduct a sociometric activity with the class in order to determine which peer(s) would most prefer to interact with the student in tutoring situations.

21. Make certain the student demonstrates appropriate behavior in tutoring situations prior to pairing him/her with a peer.

22. Make certain that the student understands that interacting with a peer(s) in tutoring situations is contingent upon appropriate behavior.

23. Supervise tutoring situations closely in order that the peer(s) with whom the student works does not stimulate inappropriate behavior.

24. Make certain that the tutoring situation is not so overstimulating as to make successful interactions with other peers difficult.

25. Reduce the emphasis on competition. Fear of failure may stimulate inappropriate behavior in tutoring situations.

26. Teach the student problem-solving skills in order that he/she may better deal with problems that may occur in interactions with other peer(s) in tutoring situations (e.g., talking, walking away, calling upon an arbitrator, compromising, etc.).

27. Find a peer with whom the student is most likely to be able to successfully interact in tutoring situations (e.g., a student with similar interests, background, ability, behavior patterns, etc.).

28. Structure the activities of the tutoring situation according to the needs/abilities of the student (e.g., establish rules, limit the stimulation of the activity, limit the length of the activity, consider the time of day, etc.).

29. Have the student practice appropriate interactions with the teacher in tutoring situations.

30. Select nonacademic activities designed to enhance appropriate interaction of the student and peer(s) (e.g., board games, model building, coloring, etc.).

31. Through interviews with other students and observations, determine those characteristics of the student which interfere with successful interactions during tutoring situations in order to determine skills or behaviors the student needs to develop for successful interactions.

32. Limit opportunities for interaction in tutoring situations on those occasions when the student is not likely to be successful (e.g., the student has experienced academic or social failure prior to the scheduled tutoring activity).

33. Make certain the student is able to successfully engage in the tutoring activity (e.g., the student understands the rules, the student is familiar with the activity, the student will be compatible with the other students engaged in the free time activity, etc.).

34. Make certain the student understands that failing to interact appropriately with a peer(s) during tutoring activities may result in removal from the activity and/or loss of participation in future activities.

35. Have the student engage in the peer tutoring situation for short periods of time, and gradually increase the length of time as the student demonstrates success.

36. Provide an appropriate location for the tutoring situation (e.g., quiet corner of the classroom, near the teacher's desk, etc.).

37. Have the student and peer tutor use the "Who, What, Where, When, How, and Why" format while completing assignments. This will help simplify and clarify concepts. (See Appendix for Outline Form.)

38 Does not take notes during class when necessary

1. Reinforce the student for taking notes during class when necessary: (a) give the student a tangible reward (e.g., classroom privileges, line leading, passing out materials, five minutes free time, etc.) when he/she takes notes during class when necessary, or (b) give the student an intangible reward (e.g., praise, handshake, smile, etc.) for taking notes during class when necessary.

2. Speak to the student to explain: (a) what he/she is doing wrong (e.g., failing to take notes) and (b) what he/she should be doing (e.g., taking notes).

3. Establish classroom rules (e.g., take notes when necessary, work on task, work quietly, remain in your seat, finish task, meet task expectations). Reiterate rules often and reinforce students for following rules.

4. Reinforce those students in the classroom who take notes during class when necessary.

5. Reinforce the student for taking notes during class when necessary based on the length of time he/she can be successful. Gradually increase the length of time required for reinforcement as the student demonstrates success.

6. Write a contract with the student specifying what behavior is expected (e.g., taking notes) and what reinforcement will be made available when the terms of the contract have been met.

7. Communicate with parents (e.g., notes home, phone calls, etc.) in order to share information concerning the student's progress and so that they may reinforce the student at home for taking notes during class when necessary.

8. Evaluate the appropriateness of note taking to determine: (a) if the task is too difficult, and (b) if the length of time scheduled to complete the task is appropriate.

9. Identify a peer to act as a model for the student to imitate appropriate note taking during class when necessary.

10. Have the student question any directions, explanations, instructions he/she does not understand.

11. Teach the student note-taking skills (e.g., copy main ideas from the board, identify main ideas from lectures, condense statements into a few key words, etc.).

12. Provide a standard format for note taking of directions or explanations (e.g., have paper and pencil or pen ready, listen for the steps in directions or explanations, write a shortened form of directions or explanations, ask to have any steps repeated when necessary, etc.).

13. Provide a standard format for lecture note taking (e.g., have paper and pencil or pen ready, listen for main ideas or important information, write a shortened form of main ideas or important information, ask to have any main ideas or important information repeated when necessary, etc.).

14. While delivering instructions, directions, lectures, etc., point out to the student that information should be written in the form of notes.

15. Have the student practice legible manuscript or cursive handwriting during simulated and actual note-taking activities.

16. Have the student keep his/her notes organized in a folder for each subject or activity.

17. Check the student's notes before he/she begins an assignment in order to determine if they are correct and adequate for the assignment.

18. Provide the student with an outline or questions to be completed during teacher delivery of instructions, directions, lectures, etc.

19. Provide the student with samples of notes taken from actual instructions, directions, lectures, etc., given in the classroom in order that he/she may learn what information is necessary for note taking.

20. Make certain the student is in the best location in the classroom to receive information for note taking (e.g., near the board, teacher, or other source of information).

21. Make certain the teacher can easily provide supervision of the student's note taking.

22. Make certain to maintain visibility to and from the student when delivering instructions, directions, lectures, etc., in order to enhance the likelihood of successful note taking.

23. Make certain that instructions, directions, lectures, etc., are presented clearly and loudly enough for the student to hear.

24. Match the rate of delivery of instructions, directions, lectures, etc., to the student's ability to take notes.

25. Provide the student with both verbal and written instructions.

26. Provide instructions, directions, lectures, etc., in sequential steps in order to enhance student note taking.

27. Provide delivery of information in short segments for the student to take notes. Gradually increase the length of delivery as the student experiences success in note taking.

28. Make certain that the vocabulary used in delivering instructions, directions, lectures, etc., is appropriate for the student's ability level.

29. Make certain the student has all necessary materials for note taking (e.g., paper, pencil, pen, etc.).

30. Make certain the student uses any necessary aids in order to facilitate note taking (e.g., eyeglasses, hearing aid, etc.).

31. Place the student next to a peer in order that the student can copy notes taken by the peer.

32. Make certain the student has adequate surface space on which to write when taking notes (e.g., uncluttered desk top).

33. Reduce distracting stimuli that would interfere with the student's note taking (e.g., other students talking, outdoor activities, movement in the classroom, hallway noise, etc.).

34. Present the information in the most interesting manner possible.

35. As an alternative to note taking, have the student tape record instructions, directions, lectures, etc.

36. Summarize the main points of instructions, directions, lectures, etc., for the student.

37. Have the student listen and take notes for the "Who, What, Where, When, How and Why" while concepts are presented. (See Appendix for Outline Form.)

38. Present concepts following the outline of: (1) Who, (2) What, (3) Where, (4) When, (5) How, and (6) Why.

39. Have the student prepare for tests using the "Who, What, Where, When, How and Why" method. The teacher should then test this same information. (See Appendix for Outline Form.)

40. Present directions following the outline of: (1) What, (2) How, (3) Materials, and (4) When. (See Appendix for Assignment Form.)

41. Have the student take notes when directions are being given following the "What, How, Materials, and When" format. (See Appendix for Assignment Form.)

39 Does not follow the rules of the classroom

1. Reinforce the student for following the rules of the classroom: (a) give the student a tangible reward (e.g., classroom privileges, line leading, passing out materials, five minutes free time, etc.) for following the rules of the classroom, or (b) give the student an intangible reward (e.g., praise, handshake, smile, etc.) for following classroom rules.

2. Speak with the student to explain: (a) what he/she is doing wrong (e.g., failing to follow classroom rules) and (b) what he/she should be doing (e.g., following the rules of the classroom).

3. Establish classroom rules (e.g., work on task, work quietly, remain in your seat, finish task, meet task expectations). Reiterate rules often and reinforce students for following rules.

4. Reinforce those students who follow the rules of the classroom.

5. Reinforce the student for following the rules of the classroom based on the length of time he/she can be successful. Gradually increase the length of time required for reinforcement as the student demonstrates success.

6. Remove the student from the group or activity until he/she can demonstrate acceptable behavior and self-control.

7. Write a contract with the student specifying what behavior is expected (e.g., following classroom rules) and what reinforcement will be made available when the terms of the contract have been met.

8. Communicate with parents (e.g., notes home, phone calls, etc.) in order to share information concerning the student's progress and so that they may reinforce the student at home for following the rules of the classroom.

9. Evaluate the appropriateness of the assigned task to determine: (a) if the task is too difficult, and (b) if the length of time scheduled for the task is appropriate.

10. Structure the environment in such a way that the student remains active and involved while demonstrating acceptable behavior.

11. Maintain visibility to and from the student. The teacher should be able to see the student and the student should be able to see the teacher, making eye contact possible at all times.

12. Give the student preferred responsibilities.

13. Present tasks in the most interesting and attractive manner possible.

14. Maintain maximum supervision of the student, gradually decreasing supervision over time.

15. Have the student maintain a chart representing the amount of time spent following classroom rules, with reinforcement for increasing acceptable behavior.

16. Practice mobility to be frequently near the student.

17. Provide the student with many social and academic successes.

18. Provide the student with positive feedback that indicates he/she is successful.

19. Post rules in various places, including on the student's desk.

20. Make certain the student receives the information necessary to perform activities (e.g., written information, verbal directions, reminders, etc.).

21. Teach the student direction-following skills.

22. Maintain a positive and professional relationship with the student (e.g., an adversary relationship is likely to result in failure to follow directions).

23. Be a consistent authority figure (e.g., be consistent in relationship with student).

24. Provide the student with optional courses of action in order to prevent total refusal to obey teacher directives.

25. Intervene early to prevent the student's behavior from leading to contagion for other students.

26. Have the student question any directions, explanations, instructions he/she does not understand.

27. Require the student to verbalize the classroom rules at designated times throughout the day (e.g., before school, during recess, at lunch, at the end of the day, etc.).

28. Deliver directions in a step-by-step sequence.

29. Have a peer act as a model for following the rules of the classroom.

30. Interact with the student frequently to determine if directives are being followed.

31. Maintain consistency in rules, routine, and general expectations of conduct and procedure.

32. Provide the student with a list of rules and/or behavior expectations.

33. Help the student identify specific rules he/she has difficulty following and make these areas goals for behavior improvement.

34. Separate the student from the peer(s) who stimulates his/her inappropriate behavior.

35. Make certain that rules and behavior expectations are consistent throughout the school and classrooms.

1. Reinforce the student for coming to school/class: (a) give the student a tangible reward (e.g., classroom privileges, line leading, passing out materials, five minutes free time, etc.) for being present, or (b) give the student an intangible reward (e.g., praise, handshake, smile, etc.) for being present.

2. Speak with the student to explain: (a) what he/she is doing wrong (e.g., absent from school/class) and (b) what he/she should be doing (e.g., be in attendance).

3. Make certain the student is appropriately placed in those classes in which he/she is enrolled (e.g., the class is not too difficult).

4. Reinforce those students who come to school/class.

5. Write a contract with the student specifying what behavior is expected (e.g., being in attendance) and what reinforcement will be made available when the terms of the contract have been met.

6. Communicate with the parents (e.g., notes home, phone calls, etc.) in order to share information concerning the student's progress and so that they may reinforce the student at home for attending school and class.

7. Reduce the emphasis on competition. Repeated failure may cause the student to remove himself/herself from the competition by not attending school or classes.

8. Communicate with the parents, agencies, or appropriate parties in order to inform them of the problem, determine the cause of the problem, and consider possible solutions to the problem.

9. Record or chart attendance with the student.

10. Begin the day or class with a success-oriented activity which is likely to be enjoyable for the student.

11. Give the student a preferred responsibility to be performed at the beginning of each day or each class.

12. Reinforce the student for getting on the bus or leaving home on time.

13. Help the student develop friendships which may encourage his/her attendance at school/class.

14. Provide the student with as many high-interest activities as possible.

15. Involve the student in extra-curricular activities.

16. Provide the student with many social and academic successes.

17. Provide the student with academic activities in the most attractive and interesting manner possible.

18. Require that the student's attendance be documented by his/her teachers (e.g., have teachers sign an attendance card).

19. Interact often with the student in a positive manner throughout the day.

20. Collect anecdotal information on the student's absent behavior. If a trend can be determined, remove the student from the situation, modify the situation, or help the student develop the skills to be more successful in the situation.

21. Have the parent bring the student to school.

22. Have a responsible peer walk to school/class with the student.

23. Establish a time for the student to leave his/her home in the morning.

24. Require that time spent away from school/class be made up at recess, during lunch, or after school.

25. Have the student document his/her attendance at the end of each school day (e.g., have the student maintain a record of attendance in the special education classroom, office, etc., and fill in the data at the end of each day).

41 Has unexcused tardiness

1. Reinforce the student for coming to an activity at the specified time: (a) give the student a tangible reward (e.g., classroom privileges, line leading, passing out materials, five minutes free time, etc.) when he/she comes to an activity at the specified time, or (b) give the student an intangible reward (e.g., praise, handshake, smile, etc.) for coming to an activity at the specified time.

2. Speak to the student to explain: (a) what he/she is doing wrong (e.g., coming late to an activity) and (b) what he/she should be doing (e.g., coming to an activity at the specified time).

3. Establish classroom rules (e.g., come to class on time, work on task, work quietly, remain in your seat, finish task, meet task expectations). Reiterate rules often and reinforce students for following rules.

4. Reinforce those students in the classroom who come to an activity at the specified time.

5. Reinforce the student for coming to an activity within a given period of time. Gradually reduce the length of time the student has to come to an activity as he/she becomes more successful at being punctual.

6. Write a contract with the student specifying what behavior is expected (e.g., coming to school on time) and what reinforcement will be made available when the terms of the contract have been met.

7. Communicate with parents (e.g., notes home, phone calls, etc.) in order to share information concerning the student's progress and so that they may reinforce the student at home for going to activities at the specified time at school.

8. Evaluate the appropriateness of the task to determine: (a) if the task is too difficult, and (b) if the length of time scheduled to complete the task is appropriate.

9. Identify a peer to act as a model for the student to imitate arriving at an activity at the specified time.

10. Provide the student with a Schedule of Daily Events in order that he/she will know which activities to attend and their times. (See Appendix for Schedule of Daily Events.)

11. Make certain that the student's daily schedule follows an established routine.

12. Limit the number of interruptions in the student's schedule.

13. Make certain the student has adequate time to get to an activity.

14. Make certain that the student knows how to get from one activity to another.

15. Use a timer as a signal to help the student get to activities at specified times.

16. Give the student a specific responsibility to be performed at the beginning of each activity in order to encourage him/her to be on time.

17. Provide the student with verbal cues when it is time to change activities (e.g., "It is time for the red group to have reading." "Now it is time for the red group to put away materials and move to the next activity." etc.).

18. Determine why the student is not arriving at activities at the specified times and modify/adjust to eliminate this problem.

19. Ask the student why he/she is not arriving at activities at the specified times. The student may have the most accurate perception as to why he/she is not arriving at activities at the specified times.

20. Help the student understand that it is permissible to leave work unfinished and return to it at a later time.

21. Determine if there are aspects of activities that the student dislikes. Remove, reduce, or modify the unpleasant aspects of activities in order to encourage the student to be on time for and participate in activities.

22. Make the student responsible for time missed (i.e., if the student misses five minutes of an activity, he/she must make up the time during recess, lunch, or other desired activities).

23. Have a peer accompany the student to activities.

24. Make certain that the student is successful at school-related activities. The student will be more likely to be on time for activities in which he/she experiences success.

25. Make the student a leader of the activity or group.

26. Make certain that other students do not make it unpleasant for the student to attend activities.

27. Make certain the student has all necessary materials for activities.

28. Record or chart promptness with the student.

29. Begin activities with a task that is highly reinforcing to the student.

30. Give the student a preferred responsibility to be performed at the beginning of each activity.

31. Assess the appropriateness of the degree of difficulty of the task in comparison with the student's ability to perform the task successfully.

32. Provide the student with as many high-interest activities as possible.

33. Provide the student with many social and academic successes.

34. Introduce academic activities in the most attractive manner possible to the student.

42 Does not check completed work for accuracy

1. Establish general rules for the classroom (e.g., be in attendance, be on time, be productive, be accurate, follow classroom rules). Reiterate rules often and reinforce students for following rules.

2. Identify a peer to serve as a model for the student in checking his/her work for accuracy.

3. Maintain mobility throughout the classroom to monitor the student checking his/her work for accuracy.

4. Provide the student with self-checking materials to check his/her work for accuracy.

5. Offer the student assistance frequently throughout the day in checking his/her work for accuracy.

6. Make certain that the student is assigned short enough tasks in order that he/she can complete assignments in time to check for accuracy. Gradually increase the length of the assignments as the student demonstrates success.

7. Allow the student additional time to complete assignments and check his/her work for accuracy.

8. Provide the student with step-by-step written directions for performing assignments. Make certain that the last directive is to check work for accuracy.

9. Require that work not checked for accuracy must be checked at another time (e.g., break time, recreational time, after school, etc.).

10. Reinforce those students in the classroom who check their work for accuracy.

11. Reinforce the student for checking his/her work for accuracy: (a) give the student a tangible reward (e.g., classroom privileges, line leading, passing out materials, five minutes free time, etc.) when he/she checks work for accuracy, or (b) give the student an intangible reward (e.g., praise, handshake, smile, etc.) when he/she checks work for accuracy.

12. Speak with the student to explain: (a) what he/she is doing wrong (e.g., not checking work for accuracy), and (b) what he/she should be doing (e.g., checking work for accuracy).

13. Check a few problems with the student to serve as a model for checking his/her work for accuracy.

14. Reinforce the student for checking work for accuracy based on the number of times he/she can be successful. Gradually increase the number of times required for reinforcement as the student demonstrates success.

15. Write a contract with the student specifying what behavior is expected (e.g., checking work for accuracy) and what reinforcement will be made available when the terms of the contract have been met.

16. Evaluate the appropriateness of the task to determine: (a) if the task is too difficult, and (b) if the length of time scheduled to complete the task is appropriate.

17. Have the student question any directions, explanations, and instructions he/she does not understand.

18. Assess the quality and clarity of directions, explanations, and instructions given to the student.

19. Structure the environment in such a way as to provide the student with increased opportunity for checking his/her work for accuracy.

20. Have the student maintain a record (e.g., chart or graph) of his/her performance in checking work for accuracy.

21. Communicate clearly to the student when it is time to check his/her work for accuracy.

22. Reinforce the student for beginning, working on, and completing assignments; and checking work for accuracy.

23. Give the student a list of specific strategies for checking the accuracy of completed work. Some specific strategies are: (1) Check math problems with the inverse operation. (2) Check language assignments for capitalization, punctuation, and neatness. (3) Use the dictionary to check spelling in written work. (4) Check spelling quizzes for careless errors. (5) Check written paragraphs using the "Who, What, Where, When, How, and Why" format. (6) Check tests and quizzes for careless errors and omitted or incomplete answers.

24. Provide the student with clearly stated written directions for homework in order that someone at home may be able to provide assistance in checking work for accuracy.

25. Provide time at school for checking homework for accuracy if homework has not been checked. (The student's failure to check homework for accuracy may be the result of variables in the home over which he/she has no control.)

26. Identify resource personnel from whom the student may receive additional assistance in checking work for accuracy (e.g., librarian, special education teacher, paraprofessional, etc.).

27. Deliver reinforcement for any and all measures of improvement in checking work for accuracy.

28. Provide the student with opportunities for checking work for accuracy prior to grading assignments.

29. Monitor student performance in order to detect errors and determine where learning problems exist.

30. Allow/require the student to make corrections after assignments have been checked the first time.

31. Provide the student with evaluative feedback for assignments completed (i.e., identify what the student did successfully, what errors were made, and what should be done to correct the errors).

32. Allow the student to put an assignment away and return to it at a later time to check for accuracy.

33. Assign a peer or volunteer to help the student check work for accuracy.

43 Does not follow written directions

1. Reinforce the student for following written directions: (a) give the student a tangible reward (e.g., classroom privileges, line leading, passing out materials, five minutes free time, etc.) when he/she appropriately follows written directions, or (b) give the student an intangible reward (e.g., praise, handshake, smile, etc.) for appropriately following written directions.

2. Speak to the student to explain: (a) what he/she is doing wrong (e.g., ignoring written directions) and (b) what he/she should be doing (e.g., following written directions).

3. Establish classroom rules (e.g., work on task, work quietly, remain in your seat, finish task, meet task expectations). Reiterate rules often and reinforce students for following rules.

4. Reinforce those students in the classroom who follow written directions.

5. Reinforce the student for following written directions based on the length of time he/she can be successful. Gradually increase the length of time required for reinforcement as the student demonstrates success.

6. Write a contract with the student specifying what behavior is expected (e.g., following written directions) and what reinforcement will be made available when the terms of the contract have been met.

7. Communicate with parents (e.g., notes home, phone calls, etc.) in order to share information concerning the student's progress and so that they may reinforce the student at home for following written directions at school.

8. Evaluate the appropriateness of the task to determine: (a) if the task is too difficult, and (b) if the length of time scheduled to complete the task is appropriate.

9. Identify a peer to act as a model for the student to imitate appropriate following of written directions.

10. Have the student question any written directions, explanations, instructions he/she does not understand.

11. Assign a peer to work with the student to help him/her follow written directions.

12. Teach the student skills for following of written directions (e.g., read carefully, write down important points, ask for clarification, wait until all directions are received before beginning, etc.).

13. Give directions in a variety of ways to increase the probability of understanding (e.g., if the student fails to understand written directions, present them in verbal form).

14. Provide clearly stated written directions (e.g., make the directions as simple and concrete as possible).

15. Reduce distracting stimuli in order to increase the student's ability to follow written directions (e.g., place the student on the front row, provide a carrel or "office" space away from distractions, etc.). This is used as a means of reducing distracting stimuli and not as a form of punishment.

16. Interact frequently with the student in order to help him/her follow written directions.

17. Structure the environment in such a way as to provide the student with increased opportunity for help or assistance on academic tasks (e.g., peer tutoring, directions for work sent home, frequent interactions, etc.).

18. Provide alternatives for the traditional format of presenting written directions (e.g., tape record directions, summarize directions, directions given by peers, etc.).

19. Assess the quality and clarity of written directions, explanations, and instructions given to the student.

20. Practice the following of written directions on nonacademic tasks (e.g., recipes, games, etc.).

21. Have the student repeat written directions orally to the teacher.

22. Reduce written directions to individual steps (e.g., give the student each additional step after completion of the previous step).

23. Deliver a predetermined signal (e.g., clapping hands, turning lights off and on, etc.) before giving written directions.

24. Deliver written directions before handing out materials.

25. Require that assignments done incorrectly, for any reason, be redone.

26. Make certain the student achieves success when following written directions.

27. Reduce the emphasis on competition. Competitive activities may cause the student to hurry to begin the task without following written directions.

28. Have the student maintain a record (e.g., chart or graph) of his/her performance in following written directions.

29. Follow a less desirable task with a highly desirable task, making the completion of the first necessary to perform the second.

30. Prevent the student from becoming over-stimulated by an activity (e.g., frustrated, angry, etc.).

31. Require the student to wait until the teacher gives him/her a signal to begin an activity after receiving written directions (e.g., hand signal, bell ringing, etc.).

32. Make certain that the student is attending to the teacher (e.g., making eye contact, hands free of writing materials, looking at assignment, etc.) before giving written directions.

33. Maintain visibility to and from the student. The teacher should be able to see the student in order to make certain the student is attending to written directions.

34. Make certain that written directions are presented on the student's reading level.

35. Present directions in both written and verbal form.

36. Provide the student with a copy of written directions at his/her desk rather than on the chalkboard, posted in the classroom, etc.

37. Tape record directions for the student to listen to individually and repeat as necessary.

38. Develop assignments/activities for the following of written directions (e.g., informal activities designed to have the student carry out directions in steps, increasing the degree of difficulty).

39. Maintain consistency in the format of written directions.

40. Have a peer help the student with any written directions he/she does not understand.

41. Seat the student close to the source of the written directions (e.g., chalkboard, projector, etc.).

42. Make certain that the print is large enough to increase the likelihood of following written directions.

43. Transfer directions from texts and workbooks when pictures or other stimuli make it difficult to attend to or follow written directions.

44. Work the first problem or problems with the student to make certain that he/she follows the written directions accurately.

45. Have the student carry out written directions one step at a time, checking with the teacher to make certain that each step is successfully followed before attempting the next.

46. Make certain that directions are given at a level at which the student can be successful (e.g., two-step or three-step directions should not be given to students who can only successfully follow one-step directions).

47. Use visual cues such as *green dot* to start, *red dot* to stop, arrows, etc., in written directions.

48. Highlight, circle, or underline key words in written directions (e.g., key words such as *match, circle, underline*, etc.).

44 Does not follow verbal directions

1. Reinforce the student for following verbal directions: (a) give the student a tangible reward (e.g., classroom privileges, line leading, passing out materials, five minutes free time, etc.) when he/she appropriately follows verbal directions, or (b) give the student an intangible reward (e.g., praise, handshake, smile, etc.) for appropriately following verbal directions.

2. Speak to the student to explain: (a) what he/she is doing wrong (e.g., ignoring verbal directions) and (b) what he/she should be doing (e.g., listening to and following verbal directions).

3. Establish classroom rules (e.g., work on task, work quietly, remain in your seat, finish task, meet task expectations). Reiterate rules often and reinforce students for following rules.

4. Reinforce those students in the classroom who follow verbal directions.

5. Reinforce the student for following verbal directions based on the length of time he/she can be successful. Gradually increase the length of time required for reinforcement as the student demonstrates success.

6. Write a contract with the student specifying what behavior is expected (e.g., following verbal directions) and what reinforcement will be made available when the terms of the contract have been met.

7. Communicate with parents (e.g., notes home, phone calls, etc.) in order to share information concerning the student's progress and so that they may reinforce the student at home for following verbal directions at school.

8. Evaluate the appropriateness of the task to determine: (a) if the task is too difficult, and (b) if the length of time scheduled to complete the task is appropriate.

9. Identify a peer to act as a model for the student to imitate appropriate following of verbal directions.

10. Have the student question any verbal directions, explanations, instructions he/she does not understand.

11. Teach the student skills for following verbal directions (e.g., listen carefully, write down important points, use environmental cues, wait until all directions are received before beginning, etc.).

12. Give directions in a variety of ways in order to increase the probability of understanding (e.g., if the student fails to understand verbal directions, present them in written form).

13. Provide clearly stated verbal directions (e.g., make the directions as simple and concrete as possible).

14. Reduce distracting stimuli in order to increase the student's ability to follow verbal directions (e.g., place the student on the front row, provide a carrel or "office" space away from distractions, etc.). This is used as a means of reducing distracting stimuli and not as a form of punishment.

15. Interact frequently with the student in order to help him/her follow verbal directions.

16. Structure the environment in such a way as to provide the student with increased opportunity for help or assistance on academic tasks (e.g., peer tutoring, directions for work sent home, frequent interactions, etc.).

17. Provide alternatives for the traditional format of presenting verbal directions (e.g., tape record directions, summarize directions, directions given by peers, etc.).

18. Assess the quality and clarity of verbal directions, explanations and instructions given to the student.

19. Have the student practice following verbal directions on nonacademic tasks (e.g., recipes, games, etc.).

20. Have the student repeat directions or give an interpretation after receiving verbal directions.

21. Reduce verbal directions to steps (e.g., give the student each additional step after completion of the previous step).

22. Deliver a predetermined signal (e.g., clapping hands, turning lights off and on, etc.) before giving verbal directions.

23. Give verbal directions before handing out materials.

24. Require that assignments done incorrectly, for any reason, be redone.

25. Make certain the student achieves success when following verbal directions.

26. Reduce emphasis on competition. Competitive activities may cause the student to hurry to begin the task without following verbal directions.

27. Have the student maintain a record (e.g., chart or graph) of his/her performance in following verbal directions.

28. Communicate clearly to the student when it is time to listen to verbal directions.

29. Provide the student with a predetermined signal when he/she is not following verbal directions (e.g., lights turned off and on, hand signals, etc.).

30. Follow a less desirable task with a highly desirable task, making the following of verbal directions and completion of the first task necessary to perform the second.

31. Prevent the student from becoming over-stimulated by an activity (e.g., frustrated, angry, etc.).

32. Make certain the student has all the materials needed to perform the assignment/activity.

33. Require the student to wait until the teacher gives him/her a signal to begin the task (e.g., hand signal, ring bell, etc.).

34. Make certain the student is attending to the teacher (e.g., making eye contact, hands free of writing materials, looking at assignment, etc.) before giving verbal directions.

35. Stand next to the student when giving verbal directions.

36. Maintain visibility to and from the student. The teacher should be able to see the student and the student should be able to see the teacher, making eye contact possible at all times when giving verbal directions.

37. Make certain that verbal directions are delivered in a nonthreatening manner (e.g., positive voice, facial expression, language, etc.).

38. Make certain that verbal directions are delivered in a supportive rather than threatening manner (e.g., "Will you please . . ." or "You need . . ." rather than "You better . . ." or "If you don't . . .").

39. Present directions in both written and verbal form.

40. Provide the student with a written copy of verbal directions.

41. Tape record directions for the student to listen to individually and repeat as necessary.

42. Maintain consistency in the format of verbal directions.

43. Develop assignments/activities for the following of verbal directions (e.g., informal activities designed to have the student carry out verbal directions in steps, increasing the degree of difficulty).

44. Have a designated person be the only individual to deliver verbal directions to the student.

45. Have a peer help the student with any verbal directions he/she does not understand.

46. Seat the student close to the source of the verbal directions (e.g., teacher, aide, peer, etc.).

47. Seat the student far enough away from peers in order to insure increased opportunities for attending to verbal directions.

48. Work the first problem or problems with the student in order to make certain that he/she follows the verbal directions accurately.

49. Work through the steps of the verbal directions as they are delivered in order to make certain the student follows the directions accurately.

50. Have the student carry out one step of the verbal directions at a time, checking with the teacher to make certain that each step is successfully followed before attempting the next.

1. Speak to the student to explain: (a) what he/she is doing wrong (e.g., failing to bring necessary materials for specified activities) and (b) what he/she should be doing (e.g., having necessary materials for specified activities).

2. Establish classroom rules (e.g., have necessary materials, work on task, work quietly, remain in your seat, finish task, and meet task expectations). Reiterate rules often and reinforce students for following rules.

3. Reinforce the student for being organized/prepared for specified activities based on the number of times he/she can be successful. Gradually increase the number of times required for reinforcement as the student demonstrates success.

4. Write a contract with the student specifying what behavior is expected (e.g., having necessary materials for specified activities) and what reinforcement will be made available when the terms of the contract have been met.

5. Evaluate the appropriateness of the task to determine: (a) if the task is too difficult, and (b) if the length of time scheduled to complete the task is appropriate.

6. Identify a peer to act as a model for the student to imitate being organized/prepared for specified activities.

7. Have the student question any directions, explanations, instructions he/she does not understand.

8. Assign a peer to accompany the student to specified activities in order to make certain the student has the necessary materials.

9. Provide the student with a list of necessary materials for each activity of the day.

10. Provide the student with verbal reminders of necessary materials required for each activity.

11. Provide time at the beginning of each day for the student to organize his/her materials.

12. Provide time at various points throughout the day for the student to organize his/her materials (e.g., before school, during recess, at lunch, at the end of the day, etc.).

13. Provide storage space for materials the student is not using at any particular time.

14. Act as a model for being organized/prepared for specified activities.

15. Make certain that work not completed because necessary materials were not brought to the specified activity must be completed during recreational or break time.

16. Have the student chart the number of times he/she is organized/prepared for specified activities.

17. Remind the student at the end of the day when materials are required for specified activities for the next day (e.g., by a note sent home, verbal reminder, etc.).

18. Have the student establish a routine to follow before coming to class (e.g., check which activity is next, determine what materials are necessary, collect materials, etc.).

19. Have the student leave necessary materials at specified activity areas.

20. Provide the student with a container in which to carry necessary materials for specified activities (e.g., backpack, book bag, briefcase, etc.).

21. Provide adequate transition time between activities for the student to organize his/her materials.

22. Establish a routine to be followed for organization and appropriate use of work materials. Provide the routine for the student in written form or verbally reiterate often.

23. Provide adequate time for the completion of activities.

24. Assess the quality and clarity of directions, explanations, and instructions given to the student.

25. Provide the student with structure for all academic activities (e.g., specific directions, routine format for tasks, time units, etc.).

26. Minimize materials needed for specified activities.

27. Provide an organizer for materials inside the student's desk.

28. Provide the student with an organizational checklist (e.g., routine activities, materials needed, and steps to follow).

29. Make certain that all personal property is labeled with the student's name.

30. Teach the student how to conserve rather than waste materials (e.g., amount of glue, paper, tape, etc., to use; putting lids, caps, tops on such materials as markers, pens, bottles, jars, cans, etc.).

31. Teach the student to maintain care of personal property and school materials (e.g., keep property with him/her, know where property is at all times, secure property in lockers, leave valuable property at home, etc.).

32. Provide the student with an appropriate place to store/secure personal property (e.g., desk, locker, closet, etc.) and require that the student store all property when not in use.

33. Limit the student's freedom to take property from school if he/she is unable to remember to return such items.

34. Make certain that failure to have necessary materials results in loss of opportunity to participate in activities or a failing grade for that day's activity.

35. Provide the student with more work space (e.g., a larger desk or table at which to work).

36. Reduce the number of materials for which the student is responsible. Increase the number as the student demonstrates appropriate use of property.

37. Require that lost or damaged property be replaced by the student. If the student cannot replace the property, restitution can be made by working at school.

38. Make certain that the student is not inadvertently reinforced for losing materials. Provide the student with used materials, copies of the materials, etc., rather than new materials if he/she fails to care for the materials in an appropriate manner.

39. Reduce distracting stimuli (e.g., place the student in the front row, provide a carrel or quiet place away from distractions, etc.). This is used as a means of reducing distracting stimuli and not as a form of punishment.

40. Interact frequently with the student in order to prompt organizational skills and appropriate use of materials.

41. Assign the student organizational responsibilities in the classroom (e.g., organizing equipment, software, materials, etc.).

42. Limit the student's use of materials (i.e., provide the student with only those materials necessary at any given time).

43. Act as a model for organization and appropriate use of work materials (e.g., putting materials away before getting others out, having a place for all materials, maintaining an organized desk area, following a schedule for the day, etc.).

44. Have the student maintain an assignment notebook which indicates those materials needed for each activity.

45. Provide the student with a Schedule of Daily Events in order that he/she knows exactly what and how much there is to do in a day. (See Appendix for Schedule of Daily Events.)

46. Supervise the student while he/she is performing schoolwork in order to monitor quality.

47. Allow natural consequences to occur as the result of the student's inability to organize or use materials appropriately (e.g., work not done during work time must be made up during recreational time, materials not maintained will be lost or not serviceable, etc.).

48. Assist the student in beginning each task in order to reduce impulsive behavior.

49. Provide a color-coded organizational system (e.g., notebook, folders, etc.).

50. Teach the student to prioritize assignments (e.g., according to importance, length, etc.).

51. Provide adequate time for completion of activities.

52. Develop monthly calendars to keep track of important events, due dates, assignments, etc.

53. Have the student use an assignment form in order to be sure all materials needed are listed. (See Appendix for Assignment Form.)

54. Require the student to use the daily Assignment Sheet with both teacher and parent signatures. (See Appendix for Assignment Sheet.)

55. Have a peer remind the student of the necessary materials required for specified activities.

56. Provide the student with enough materials to satisfy his/her immediate needs (e.g., one of everything). Gradually reduce the number of materials over time, requiring the student to bring materials as he/she becomes more successful at doing so.

46 Does not demonstrate appropriate use of school-related materials

1. Speak to the student to explain: (a) what he/she is doing wrong (e.g., failing to use school-related materials appropriately) and (b) what he/she should be doing (e.g., using school-related materials as directed).

2. Establish classroom rules (e.g., work on task, work quietly, remain in your seat, finish task, meet task expectations). Reiterate rules often and reinforce students for following rules.

3. Reinforce the student for using school-related materials appropriately based on the length of time he/she can be successful. Gradually increase the length of time required for reinforcement as the student demonstrates success.

4. Write a contract with the student specifying what behavior is expected (e.g., appropriate use of school-related materials) and what reinforcement will be made available when the terms of the contract have been met.

5. Evaluate the appropriateness of the task to determine: (a) if the task is too difficult, and (b) if the length of time scheduled to complete the task is appropriate.

6. Identify a peer to act as a model for the student to imitate appropriate use of school-related materials.

7. Have the student question any directions, explanations, instructions he/she does not understand.

8. Provide time at the beginning of each day to help the student organize his/her school-related materials.

9. Provide time at various points throughout the day to help the student organize his/her school-related materials (e.g., before school, during recess, at lunch, at the end of the day, etc.).

10. Provide the student with adequate work space (e.g., a larger desk or table at which to work).

11. Provide storage space for school-related materials the student is not using at any particular time.

12. Reduce distracting stimuli (e.g., place the student on the front row, provide a carrel or quiet place away from distractions, etc.). This is used as a means of reducing distracting stimuli and not as a form of punishment.

13. Interact frequently with the student in order to prompt organizational skills and appropriate use of school-related materials.

14. Assign the student organizational responsibilities in the classroom (e.g., organizing equipment, software, materials, etc.).

15. Limit the student's use of school-related materials (e.g., provide the student with only those school-related materials necessary at any given time).

16. Act as a model for organization and appropriate use of school-related materials (e.g., putting materials away before getting others out, having a place for all materials, maintaining an organized desk area, following a schedule for the day, etc.).

17. Provide adequate transition time between activities for the student to organize himself/herself.

18. Establish a routine to be followed for organization and appropriate use of school-related materials.

19. Provide adequate time for the completion of activities.

20. Require the student to organize his/her work area at regular intervals. (It is recommended that this be done at least three times per day.)

21. Supervise the student while he/she is performing schoolwork in order to monitor quality.

22. Allow natural consequences to occur as the result of the student's inability to organize or use school-related materials appropriately (e.g., materials not maintained appropriately will be lost or not serviceable).

23. Assess the quality and clarity of directions, explanations, and instructions given to the student.

24. Assist the student in beginning each task in order to reduce impulsive behavior.

25. Provide the student with structure for all academic activities (e.g., specific directions, routine format for tasks, time units, etc.).

26. Give the student a checklist of school-related materials necessary for each activity.

27. Minimize school-related materials needed.

28. Provide an organizer for school-related materials inside the student's desk.

29. Provide the student with an organizational checklist (e.g., routine activities and steps to follow).

30. Teach the student appropriate care of school-related materials (e.g., sharpening pencils, keeping books free of marks and tears, etc.).

31. Make certain that all of the student's school-related materials are labeled with his/her name.

32. Point out to the student that loaning his/her school-related materials to other students does not reduce his/her responsibility for the materials.

33. Teach the student to conserve rather than waste school-related materials (e.g., amount of glue, paper, tape, etc., to use; putting lids, caps, and tops on materials such as markers, pens, bottles, jars, cans, etc.).

34. Teach the student appropriate ways to deal with anger and frustration rather than destroying school-related materials.

35. Teach the student to maintain school-related materials (e.g., keep materials with him/her, know where materials are at all times, secure materials in his/her locker, etc.).

36. Provide the student with an appropriate place to store/secure school-related materials (e.g., desk, locker, closet, etc.) and require him/her to store all materials when not in use.

37. Explain to the student that the failure to care for school-related materials will result in the loss of freedom to maintain materials.

38. Provide reminders (e.g., a list of school-related materials) to help the student maintain and care for school-related materials.

39. Limit the student's freedom to take school-related materials from school if he/she is unable to return such items.

40. Provide the student with verbal reminders of school-related materials needed for each activity.

41. Limit the student's opportunity to use school-related materials if he/she is unable to care for his/her own personal property.

42. Make certain that failure to have necessary school-related materials results in loss of opportunity to participate in activities or a failing grade for that day's activity.

43. Reduce the number of school-related materials for which the student is responsible. Increase the number as the student demonstrates appropriate care of materials.

44. Teach the student safety rules in the handling of school-related materials (e.g., pencils; scissors; compass; biology, industrial arts, and home economics materials; etc.).

45. Teach the student the appropriate use of school-related materials (e.g., scissors, pencils, compass, rulers; and biology, industrial arts, and home economics materials, etc.).

46. Require that lost or damaged school-related materials be replaced by the student. If the student cannot replace the property, restitution can be made by working at school.

47. Make certain the student is not inadvertently reinforced for losing or damaging school-related materials. Provide the student with used or damaged materials, copies of the materials, etc., rather than new materials.

47 Does not demonstrate an effective organizational system when completing homework assignments

1. Identify a particular place to study that is free of clutter (e.g., desk, table, etc.).

2. Identify and use a place to study that is quiet and free from movement or other distractions (e.g., no radio or television, away from siblings, isolated from discussions or telephone calls).

3. Choose a time for studying that allows for maximum concentration. This will be an individual preference (e.g., after school, after one hour of play and relaxation, after dinner, etc.).

4. Have the student study at the same identified time each day. In the event he/she does not have an assignment, he/she should use this time for reading or reviewing.

5. Provide the student with needed materials in order to be organized at his/her work area (e.g., paper, pencils, pens, ruler, eraser, pencil sharpener, tape, crayons, colored pencils, scissors, stapler, dictionary, thesaurus). This will reduce the need for the student to interrupt his/her own work to look for materials.

6. Keep the identified work area at a comfortable room temperature. A room kept too warm will make the student drowsy.

7. Have the student prioritize his/her assignments on the basis of due dates, then he/she should divide study time according to assignments. (See Appendix for Assignment Sheet and Schedule of Daily Events.)

8. As a parent, be available for help or to check for completion and/or accuracy of homework. Being available does not mean sitting with the student. It is best to be in another room while still available.

9. For lengthy projects, have the student break the assignment into manageable steps, completing one step each night (e.g., information gathering, organizing information, writing introduction, etc.). (See Using the Study Skills Guide for 2-Week Project Outline Sample.)

10. It is vital that the student be required to follow a routine of studying and preparing for school each day.

11. Have the student plan for short study breaks (e.g., drink of water, stretching break, restroom break, etc.).

12. Have extra reading material available at the study area to read when assignments are complete.

13. Require the student to review nightly for two to three nights before a test.

14. Require the student to study graphics, pictures and captions within chapters.

15. After reading a chapter, require the student to summarize the chapter with his/her parent using the Outline Form. (See Appendix.)

16. When reading for content, require the student to answer "Who, What, Where, When, How and Why" using the Outline Form. (See Appendix.)

17. Require the student to use the Flash Card Study Aid when preparing for tests. (See Appendix.)

18. If the student regularly has difficulty remembering to take necessary materials home, a set of school texts can be kept at home for his/her use (e.g., spelling book, reading book, science book, etc.).

19. Require that the student note deadlines for assignments on an Assignment Sheet with both teacher and parent signatures. (See Appendix for Assignment Sheet.)

20. Require the student to use the same structure for all academic activities (e.g., routine format for tasks, time, etc.).

21. Provide an organizer for materials inside the student's desk.

22. Make sure the student is aware of those specified times when he/she can watch television, visit with a friend, etc.

23. At the end of each study period, require the student to show a parent his/her progress on assignments.

48 Fails to correctly solve math problems requiring addition

1. Provide the student with a quiet place to work (e.g., "office," study carrel, etc.). This is used as a means of reducing distracting stimuli and not as a form of punishment.

2. Have the student solve addition problems by manipulating objects and by stating the process(es) used.

3. Discuss and provide the student with a list of words/phrases which indicate an addition operation in word problems (e.g., *together, altogether, sum, in all, both, gained, received, total, saved*, etc.).

4. Assign a peer to act as a model for the student and to demonstrate how to solve addition problems.

5. Provide the student with many concrete experiences to help him/help learn and remember math facts. Use popsicle sticks, tongue depressors, paper clips, buttons, fingers, etc., to form groupings to teach addition facts.

6. Have the student use a calculator to reinforce learning addition. Have the student solve several problems each day using a calculator.

7. Provide practice of addition facts using computer software programs that give immediate feedback to the student.

8. Use daily drill activities to help the student memorize addition facts (e.g., written problems, flash cards, etc.).

9. Have the student use a number line attached to his/her desk to solve addition problems.

10. Have the student use a calculator for drill activities of basic addition facts.

11. Find opportunities for the student to apply addition facts to real-life situations (e.g., getting change in the cafeteria, measuring the lengths of objects in industrial arts, etc.).

12. Have the student perform timed drills in addition to reinforce basic math facts. The student "competes" against his/her own best time.

13. Develop a math facts reference sheet for addition for the student to use at his/her desk when solving math problems.

14. Have the student independently solve half of his/her addition facts/problems each day, allow the use of a calculator as reinforcement to solve the rest of the problems.

15. Make certain the student understands number concepts and the relationship of number symbols to numbers of objects before requiring him/her to solve math problems requiring addition.

16. Make certain the student knows the concepts of *more than, less than, equal*, and *zero*. The use of tangible objects will facilitate the learning process.

17. Have the student make sets of objects and add the sets together to obtain a sum total.

18. Provide the student with opportunities for tutoring from peers or teacher. Allow the student to tutor others when he/she has mastered a concept.

19. Reinforce the student for attempting and completing work. Emphasize the number correct, then encourage him/her to see how many more he/she can correct without help. Have the student maintain his/her own "private" chart of math performance.

20. Provide the student with enjoyable math activities during free time in the classroom (e.g., computer games, math games, manipulatives, etc.).

21. Have the student check all math work. Reinforce the student for each error he/she corrects.

22. Allow the student to perform alternative assignments. Gradually introduce more components of the regular assignments until those assignments can be performed successfully by the student.

23. Make certain that the language used to communicate with the student about addition is consistent (e.g., "Add the numbers." "What is the total?" or "Find the sum.").

24. Make certain the student has mastery of math concepts at any level before introducing a new skill level.

25. Provide the student with shorter math tasks, but give more of them throughout the day (e.g., four assignments of five problems each rather than one assignment of twenty problems).

26. Work the first problem or two of the math assignment with the student in order to make certain that he/she understands the directions and the operation necessary to solve the problem.

27. Teach the student to use resources in the environment to help him/her solve math problems (e.g., counting figures, counting numbers of objects, using a calculator, etc.).

28. Have the student talk through the math problem as he/she solves it in order to identify errors the student is making.

29. Have the student add numbers of objects. Have him/her then pair number symbols with the numbers of objects while he/she solves simple addition problems. Gradually remove the objects as the student demonstrates success in solving simple addition problems.

49 Fails to correctly solve math problems requiring subtraction

1. Provide the student with a quiet place to work (e.g., "office," study carrel, etc.). This is used as a means of reducing distracting stimuli and not as a form of punishment.

2. Have the student solve math problems by manipulating objects and by stating the process(es) used.

3. Discuss words and phrases which usually indicate subtraction operations (e.g., *difference between, from, left, how many more, how many less, how much taller, how much farther*, etc.).

4. Assign a peer to act as a model for the student to demonstrate how to solve subtraction problems.

5. Provide the student with many concrete experiences to help him/her learn and remember math facts. Use popsicle sticks, paper clips, fingers, etc., to form groupings to teach subtraction facts.

6. Have the student use a calculator to reinforce learning subtraction. Have the student solve several problems each day using a calculator.

7. Provide practice of subtraction facts using computer software programs that give immediate feedback to the student.

8. Use daily drill activities to help the student memorize subtraction facts (e.g., written problems, flash cards, etc.).

9. Have the student perform timed drills in subtraction to reinforce basic math facts. The student "competes" against his/her own best time.

10. Find opportunities for the student to apply subtraction facts to real-life situations (e.g., getting change in the cafeteria, measuring the length of objects in industrial arts, etc.).

11. Have the student use a number line attached to his/her desk to solve subtraction problems.

12. Have the student use a calculator for drill activities of basic subtraction facts.

13. Develop a math facts reference sheet for subtraction for the student to use at his/her desk when solving math problems.

14. Have the student independently solve half of his/her subtraction problems each day; allow the use of a calculator as reinforcement to solve the rest of the problems.

15. Make certain the student understands number concepts and the relationships of number symbols to numbers of objects before requiring him/her to solve math problems requiring subtraction.

16. Make certain the student knows the concepts of *more than, less than, equal*, and *zero*. The use of tangible objects will facilitate the learning process.

17. Provide the student with opportunities for tutoring from peers and teachers. Allow the student to tutor others when he/she has mastered a concept.

18. Reinforce the student for attempting and completing work. Emphasize the number correct; then encourage him/her to see how many more he/she can correct without help. Have the student maintain his/her own "private" chart of math performance.

19. Provide the student with enjoyable math activities during free time in the classroom (e.g., computer games, math games, manipulatives, etc.).

20. Have the student check all math work. Reinforce the student for each error he/she corrects.

21. Allow the student to perform alternative assignments. Gradually introduce more components of the regular assignments until those assignments can be performed successfully by the student.

22. Make certain that the language used to communicate with the student about subtraction is consistent (e.g., ''Subtract the numbers.'' ''What is the difference?'' etc.).

23. Make certain the student has mastery of math concepts at any level before introducing a new skill level.

24. Provide the student with shorter math tasks, but give more of them throughout the day (e.g., four assignments of five problems each rather than one assignment of twenty problems).

25. Work the first problem or two of the math assignment with the student in order to make certain that he/she understands the directions and the operation necessary to solve the problem.

26. Teach the student to use resources in the environment to help him/her solve math problems (e.g., counting figures, counting numbers of objects, using a calculator, etc.).

27. Have the student learn to subtract numbers of objects, then pair symbols with numbers of objects while the student solves the subtraction problem. In the last step, the student subtracts the number symbols without using objects.

28. Have the student talk through math problems as he/she solves them in order to identify errors he/she is making.

29. Require the student to check subtraction problems by adding (i.e., the difference plus the subtrahend equals the minuend). Reinforce the student for each error he/she corrects.

30. Make certain the student learns the concept of *take away* (e.g., ''You have 3 toys and I take away 2 of them. How many do you have left?'').

50 Fails to correctly solve math problems requiring multiplication

1. Provide the student with a quiet place to work (e.g., "office," study carrel, etc.). This is used as a means of reducing distracting stimuli and not as a form of punishment.

2. Reduce the emphasis on competition. Competitive activities may cause the student to hurry and do multiplication problems incorrectly.

3. Have the student solve math problems by manipulating objects and stating the process involved.

4. Discuss words/phrases which usually indicate a multiplication operation (e.g., *area, each, times, product, double, triple, twice*, etc.).

5. Assign a peer to act as a model for the student to demonstrate how to solve multiplication problems.

6. Provide the student with many concrete experiences to help him/her learn and remember math facts. Use popsicle sticks, tongue depressors, paper clips, buttons, fingers, etc., to form groupings to teach multiplication facts.

7. Have the student use a calculator to reinforce learning multiplication facts. Have the student solve several multiplication problems each day using a calculator.

8. Provide practice of multiplication facts using computer software programs that give immediate feedback to the student.

9. Use daily drill activities to help the student memorize multiplication facts (e.g., written problems, flash cards, etc.).

10. Reinforce the student for attempting and completing work. Emphasize the number correct; then encourage him/her to see how many more he/she can perform correctly without help. Have the student maintain his/her own "private" chart of math performance.

11. Have the student perform timed drills in multiplication to reinforce basic math facts. The student "competes" against his/her own best time.

12. Have the student use a calculator for drill activities of basic multiplication facts.

13. Develop a math facts reference sheet for multiplication for the student to use at his/her desk when solving math problems.

14. Have the student independently solve half of his/her multiplication problems each day; allow the use of a calculator as reinforcement to complete the other half of the assignment.

15. Make certain the student understands number concepts and the relationship of number symbols to numbers of objects before requiring him/her to solve math problems requiring multiplication.

16. Provide the student with opportunities for tutoring from peers or teachers. Allow the student to tutor others when he/she has mastered a concept.

17. Provide the student with enjoyable math activities during free time in the classroom (e.g., computer games, math games, manipulatives, etc.).

18. Allow the student to perform alternative assignments. Gradually introduce more components of the regular assignments until those assignments can be performed successfully by the student.

19. Have the student check all math work. Reinforce the student for each error he/she corrects.

20. Make certain the student has mastery of math concepts at one level before introducing a new skill level.

21. Provide the student with shorter math tasks, but give more of them throughout the day (e.g., four assignments of five problems each rather than one assignment of twenty problems).

22. Work the first problem or two of the math assignment with the student in order to make certain that he/she understands the directions and the operation necessary to solve the problems.

23. Teach the student to use resources in the environment to help him/her solve math problems (e.g., counting figures, counting numbers of objects, using a calculator, etc.).

24. Have the student talk through the math problems as he/she solves them in order to identify errors he/she is making.

25. Make certain the student understands that multiplication is a short way of adding by giving him/her examples of how much longer it takes to add than to multiply.

26. Practice skip counting with 2's, 3's and 5's.

27. Teach the student the identity element of one. Any number times one is always that number.

28. Have the student count by equal distances on a number line. Demonstrate that the equal distances represent skip counting, which is the concept of multiplication.

29. Teach the student the zero element. Any number times zero will always be zero.

30. Have the student practice the multiplication tables each day with a peer using flash cards.

31. Identify specific multiplication problems the student fails to correctly solve and target these problems for additional instruction and time to be spent in tutoring and drill activities.

51 Fails to correctly solve math problems requiring division

1. Provide the student with a quiet place to work (e.g., "office," study carrel, etc.). This is used as a means of reducing distracting stimuli and not as a form of punishment.

2. Have the student solve math problems by manipulating objects and stating the process(es) used.

3. Discuss words and phrases which usually indicate a division operation (e.g., *into, share, each, average, quotient, half as many*, etc.).

4. Assign a peer to act as a model for the student to demonstrate how to solve division problems.

5. Provide the student with many concrete experiences to help him/her learn division facts. Use popsicle sticks, tongue depressors, paper clips, buttons, fingers, etc., to form groupings to teach division facts.

6. Have the student use a calculator to reinforce learning division. Have the student solve several problems each day using a calculator.

7. Provide practice of division facts using computer software programs that give immediate feedback to the student.

8. Use daily drill activities to help the student memorize division facts (e.g., written problems, flash cards, etc.).

9. Have the student perform timed drill activities to reinforce basic math facts. The student "competes" against his/her own best time.

10. Have the student use a calculator for drill activities of basic division facts.

11. Find opportunities for the student to apply division facts to real-life situations (e.g., money, average length of time it takes to do a job, etc.).

12. Develop a math fact reference sheet for division for the student to use at his/her desk when solving math problems.

13. Have the student independently solve half of his/her math problems each day. Have the student use a calculator as reinforcement to complete the other half of the problems.

14. Make certain the student understands number concepts and the relationships of number symbols to numbers of objects before requiring him/her to solve math problems requiring division.

15. Make certain the student knows the concepts of *more than, less than, equal*, and *zero*. The use of tangible objects will facilitate the learning process.

16. Give the student several objects (e.g., one inch cubes, plastic links, etc.) and have him/her divide them into groups.

17. Provide the student with opportunities for tutoring from peers or teachers. Allow the student to tutor others when he/she has mastered a concept.

18. Reinforce the student for attempting and completing work. Emphasize the number correct; then encourage him/her to see how many more he/she can correct without help. Have the student maintain his/her own "private" chart of math performance.

19. Provide the student with enjoyable math activities during free time in the classroom (e.g., computer games, math games, manipulatives, etc.).

20. Allow the student to perform alternative versions of the assignments. Gradually introduce more components of the regular assignments until those assignments can be performed successfully.gnment

21. Make certain that the language used to communicate with the student about division is consistent (e.g., "Divide the numbers." "What is the divisor?" "What is the dividend?" etc.).

22. Have the student check all math work. Reinforce the student for each error he/she corrects.

23. Make certain the student has mastery of math concepts at any level before introducing a new skill level.

24. Provide the student with shorter math tasks, but give more of them throughout the day (e.g., four assignments of five problems each rather than one assignment of twenty problems).

25. Work the first problem or two of the assignment with the student in order to make certain that he/she understands the directions and the operation necessary to solve the problems.

26. Teach the student to use resources in the environment to help him/her solve math problems (e.g., counting figures, counting numbers of objects, using a calculator, etc.).

27. Have the student learn to divide numbers of objects; then the student pairs number symbols with numbers of objects while solving the division problem. In the last step, the student divides without using objects.

28. Have the student talk through the math problem as he/she solves it in order to identify errors the student is making.

29. Teach the student the identity element of one. Any number divided by one is always that number.

30. Have the student practice the division tables each day with a peer using flash cards.

31. Identify specific division problems the student fails to correctly solve and target problems for additional instruction and time to be spent in tutoring and drill activities.

32. Make certain the student has mastery of the concept of sets. Have the student practice dividing sets into two subsets, etc., to reinforce the concept of division.

52 Does not remember math facts

1. Beginning with the addition and subtraction facts, separate the basic facts into "sets," each to be memorized successively by the student.

2. Using the tracking technique to help the student learn math facts, present a few facts at a time. Gradually increase the number of facts the student must remember as he/she demonstrates success.

3. Provide the student with many concrete experiences to help him/her learn and remember math facts. Use popsicle sticks, tongue depressors, paper clips, buttons, etc., to form groupings to teach math facts.

4. Use fingers to teach the student to form addition and subtraction combinations. Have the student hold up fingers and add or subtract other fingers to find the correct answer.

5. Have the student use a calculator to reinforce learning of the math facts. Have the student solve several problems each day using a calculator.

6. Provide practice of math facts using computer software programs that provide immediate feedback to the student.

7. Use daily drill activities to help the student memorize math facts (e.g., written problems, flash cards, etc.).

8. Develop and post basic addition, subtraction, multiplication, and division charts, which the student can use in solving math problems.

9. Build upon math facts the student already knows, reinforcing facts the student has mastered. Add one new fact at a time as the student demonstrates success.

10. Have the student perform timed drills to reinforce basic math facts. The student "competes" against his/her own best time.

11. Have the student use a number line attached to his/her desk to add and subtract.

12. Choose one fact with which the student is unsuccessful and review it several times a day. Make that fact the student's "fact of the day."

13. Have the student complete a math facts worksheet and have him/her use a calculator to check and correct the problems.

14. Have a peer tutor work with the student each day on drill activities (e.g., flash cards).

15. Avoid going on to multiplication and division facts until addition and subtraction facts have been mastered.

16. Have the student use math fact records and tapes for math fact drill activities.

17. Use manipulative objects (e.g., pegboard, abacus, base ten blocks, etc.) to teach the student basic math facts while providing a visual image.

18. Have the student use a calculator for drill activities of basic math facts.

19. Find opportunities for the student to apply math facts to real-life situations (e.g., getting change in the cafeteria, measuring the lengths of objects in industrial arts, etc.).

20. Develop a math facts reference sheet for addition, subtraction, multiplication, or division for the student to use at his/her desk when solving math problems.

21. Have the student independently solve half of his/her math problems each day; allow the use of a calculator as reinforcement to complete the other half of the assignment.

22. Have the student reinforce multiplication facts by practicing skip counting by the number (e.g., 5's: 5, 10, 15, 20, 25, 30, etc.).

23. Have students complete a math fact quiz sheet for a daily drill as students arrive each morning.

24. If a student continues to have difficulty memorizing facts, allow him/her to keep a chart of facts at his/her desk for reference in related math problems.

25. Require the student to practice facts at home with flash cards, computer programs or games.

26. Play class games to reinforce math facts (e.g., *Bingo, Jeopardy,* teacher-made games, etc.).

27. Teach the student that once addition facts are mastered, subtraction facts are simply the inverse. The same concept holds true for multiplication and division.

28. Have the student play a math fact game with other students. Let each student take turns answering and checking facts.

29. Provide practice of math facts using a computer with software programs that provide game-like activities for reinforcement of facts.

53 Does not make use of columns when solving math problems

1. Identify a peer to act as a model for the student to demonstrate the use of columns when working math problems.

2. Use manipulative objects (e.g., base ten blocks, plastic links, etc.) to teach the student place value by providing a visual image.

3. Make certain the student has the prerequisite skills to learn place value (e.g., counting orally, understanding sets, writing numbers to 100, etc.).

4. Make certain the student knows the concepts and terminology necessary to learn place value (e.g., *set, column, middle, left, digit*, etc.).

5. Make certain the student understands that the collective value of ten *ones* is equal to one ten and that ten *tens* is equal to one hundred.

6. Provide the student with learning experiences in grouping tangible objects into groups of ones, tens, hundreds, etc.

7. Have the student practice labeling columns to represent ones, tens, hundreds, etc.

8. Have the student practice regrouping a number in different positions and determining its value (e.g., 372, 723, 237).

9. Make certain the student understands the zero concept in place value (e.g., there are no tens in the number "207," so a zero is put in the tens column).

10. Money concepts will help the student learn place value by association (e.g., $1.26 is the same as six pennies or six ones, two dimes or two tens, one dollar or one hundred).

11. Use vertical lines on graph paper to help the student visualize columns and put a single digit in each column.

12. Make certain the student understands that math problems of addition and multiplication move from right to left beginning with the ones column.

13. Provide the student with many opportunities to indicate the value of columns in multiple-digit numbers (e.g., 56= ( ) tens and ( ) ones; 329= ( ) hundreds, ( ) tens, and ( ) ones; etc.).

14. Teach the student the concept of filling each column and moving on the the next column from ones to tens, to hundreds, to thousands, etc.

15. Develop a marked column format (e.g. thousands|hundreds|tens|ones) on a master which can be copied for the student to use in solving all assigned math problems.

16. Require the student to check all his/her math assignments for accuracy. Reinforce the student for each correction made in the use of columns.

17. Have the student use a calculator to solve math problems involving the use of columns.

18. Provide the student with color-coded columns to help the student use columns accurately.

19. Provide the student with a masked window to help the student use columns accurately.

20. Have the student practice using columns when solving math problems by using a computer program which automatically chooses the correct column at input.

21. Provide the student with self-checking materials to reinforce the use of columns.

22. Have the student exchange 10 pennies for a dime and correlate that activity with grouping ten *ones* and placing a 1 in the tens column and a 0 in the ones column.

1. Make certain that the student's inability to read is not the cause of his/her difficulty in solving math word problems.

2. Have the student question any directions, explanations, or instructions he/she does not understand.

3. Provide the student with a quiet place to work (e.g., "office," study carrel, etc.). This is used as a means of reducing distracting stimuli and not as a form of punishment.

4. Have the student read the math word problem silently and then aloud and identify the mathematical operation required.

5. Provide word problems that require a one-step process, making certain that the sentences are short and concise.

6. Teach the student to look for "clue" or "key" words in word problems that indicate the mathematical operation (e.g., *in all* usually means addition, *how many are left* means subtraction, etc.).

7. Have the student orally analyze the steps that are required to solve word problems (e.g., "What is given?" "What is asked?" "What operation(s) is used?" etc.).

8. Represent numerical amounts in word problems in concrete forms (e.g., problems involving money can be represented by providing the student with the appropriate amount of real or play money).

9. Have the student write a number sentence after reading a math word problem. (This process will help the student see the numerical relationship prior to finding the answer.)

10. Ask the student to identify the primary question that must be answered to solve a given word problem. Continue this activity using more difficult word problems containing two or more questions. Make sure the student understands that questions are often implied rather than directly asked.

11. Have the student create word problems for number sentences. Place the number sentences on the chalkboard and have the student tell or write word problems that could be solved by the number sentences.

12. Have the student restate math word problems in his/her own words.

13. Have the student make up his/her own word problems. Direct the student to write problems involving specific operations. Other students in the classroom could be required to solve these problems. The student can also provide answers to his/her own problems.

14. Supplement textbook problems with teacher-made problems. These problems can deal with classroom experiences. Include students' names in the word problems to make them more realistic and meaningful to the student.

15. Use word problems that are of interest to the student and related to his/her experiences.

16. Make certain the student reads through the entire word problem before attempting to solve it.

17. Teach the student to break down each math word problem into specific steps.

18. Have the student make notes to "set the problem up" in written form as he/she reads the math word problem.

19. Have the student simulate situations which relate to math word problems (e.g., trading, selling, buying, etc.).

20. Have the student solve math word problems by manipulating objects and by stating the process(es) used.

21. Discuss words/phrases which usually indicate a subtraction operation (e.g., difference between, from, left, how many more, how many less, how much taller, how much farther, how much heavier, withdrawal, spend, lost, remain, more, etc.).

22. Discuss and provide the student with a list of words/phrases which usually indicate an addition operation (e.g., *together, altogether, sum, in all, both, gained, received, total, won, saved,* etc.).

23. Discuss words/phrases which usually indicate a multiplication operation (e.g., area, each, times, product, double, triple, twice, etc.).

24. Discuss words/phrases which usually indicate a division operation (e.g., into, share, each, average, monthly, daily, weekly, yearly, quotient, half as many, etc.).

25. Teach the student to convert words into their numerical equivalents to solve word problems (e.g., two weeks = 14 days, one-third = 1/3, one year = 12 months, one quarter = 25 cents, one yard = 36 inches, etc.).

26. Teach the student relevant vocabulary often found in math word problems (e.g., *dozen, amount, triple, twice,* etc.).

27. Allow the student to use a calculator when solving math word problems.

28. Require the student to read math word problems at least twice before beginning to solve the problems.

29. Have the student begin solving basic word problems which combine a math problem and a word problem such as:

$$7 \text{ apples}$$
$$\text{and } \underline{3 \text{ apples}}$$
$$\text{equals } 10 \text{ apples}$$

Gradually change the problems to a math word problem as the student demonstrates success.

30. Before introducing completed word problems, present the student with phrases to be translated into numbers (e.g., six less than ten equals 10 - 6).

31. Assign a peer to act as a model for the student to demonstrate how to solve math word problems.

32. Reduce the number of problems assigned to the student at one time (e.g., five problems instead of ten).

33. Demonstrate for the student how to solve math word problems by reading the problem and solving the problem one step at a time before going on to the next step.

34. Speak with the student to explain: (a) what he/she is doing wrong (e.g., using the wrong operation, failing to read the problem carefully, etc.) and (b) what he/she should be doing (e.g., using the appropriate operation, reading the problem carefully, etc.).

35. Correlate word problems with computation procedures just learned in the classroom (e.g., multiplication operations with multiplication word problems, etc.).

36. Teach the student the meaning of mathematical terms (e.g., *sum, dividend,* etc.). Frequently review the terms and their meanings.

37. Highlight or underline key words in math word problems (e.g., references to the operation involved, etc.).

38. Provide the student with a checklist to follow in solving math word problems (e.g., what information is given, what question is asked, what operation(s) is used).

55 Fails to change from one math operation to another

1. Use visual cues (e.g., stop signs or red dots) on paper when the student must change operations. Have the student raise his/her hand when reaching stop signs and provide the student with instructions for the next problem.

2. Use color coding (e.g., make addition signs green, subtraction signs red, etc.). Gradually reduce the use of colors as the student demonstrates success.

3. Reduce the number of problems on a page (e.g., five problems to a page with the student being required to do four pages of work throughout the day).

4. Make certain the student recognizes all math operation symbols (e.g., +, -, x, ÷).

5. Have the student practice recognizing series of math symbols (e.g., +, -, x, ÷).

6. Use a written reminder beside math problems to indicate which math operation is to be used (e.g., division, addition, subtraction, etc.). Gradually reduce the use of reminders as the student demonstrates success.

7. Make the math operation symbols, next to the problems, extra large in order that the student will be more likely to observe the symbol.

8. Require the student to go through math assignments highlighting or otherwise marking the operation of each problem before he/she beings to solve the math problems.

9. Work the first problem or two of a math assignment for the student in order that he/she knows which operation to use.

10. Use a separate piece of paper for each type of math problem. Gradually introduce different types of problems on the same page.

11. Have the student solve math problems using a calculator.

12. Provide the student with computer software that requires him/her to solve a variety of types of math problems.

13. Provide the student with self-checking materials to reinforce solving problems correctly.

14. Have the student estimate math solutions before solving as a tool for self-checking.

15. Provide the student with a peer tutor to solve math problems.

16. Have the student orally explain the problem to a teacher, assistant or peer before solving the problem.

56 Does not understand abstract math concepts without concrete examples

1. Have the student practice the concept of regrouping by "borrowing" and "carrying" from manipulatives arranged in columns set up like math problems.

2. Have the student use "sets" of objects from the environment to practice addition, subtraction, multiplication, and division problems.

3. Use actual change and dollar bills, clocks, etc., to teach concepts of money, telling time, etc.

4. Make certain all of the student's math problems have concrete examples associated with each one (e.g., 9 minus 7 becomes 9 apples minus 7 apples, etc.).

5. Work the first problem or two with the student, explaining how to associate concrete examples with each problem (e.g., 9 minus 7 becomes 9 apples minus 7 apples).

6. Have a peer tutor assist the student in solving math problems by providing concrete examples associated with each problem (e.g., 9 minus 7 becomes 9 apples minus 7 apples).

7. Use a scale, ruler, measuring cups, etc., to teach math concepts using measurement.

8. Make certain to use terms when speaking to the student which convey abstract concepts to describe tangible objects in the environment (e.g., larger, smaller, square, triangle, etc.).

9. Use concrete examples when teaching abstract concepts (e.g., numbers of objects to convey more than, less than; rulers and yardsticks to convey concepts of height, width, etc.).

10. Review, on a daily basis, those abstract concepts which have been previously introduced. Introduce new abstract concepts only after the student has mastery of those concepts previously presented.

11. Provide the student with computer software which uses graphics associated with math problems.

12. Have the student play games with colored chips, assigning values to each color to learn the concept of one, tens, etc.

13. Make sure that the student is taught concepts such as "square" and "cube" separately. To introduce both concepts at the same time may be confusing.

14. Provide physical objects of math concepts to teach these concepts (e.g., when referring to a yard, provide the student with a yardstick to make it concrete for him/her, etc.).

15. Provide the student with money stamps to solve money problems (e.g., penny, nickel, dime, etc.).

16. Provide the student with clock stamps that he/she fills in when practicing the concept of telling time.

17. Introduce all new abstract math concepts with a concrete example (e.g., to introduce the concept of liquid measurement, use a liquid and measuring cups with ounces indicated).

18. Have the student use concrete manipulatives in real-life problems (e.g., use measuring cups to prepare a recipe, use money to purchase items from the store).

19. Only after a student has worked with the concrete manipulatives and mastered the concept, should the abstract symbols and terms be introduced (e.g., ounce, oz.; cup, c.; pint, pt.).

20. When introducing an abstract concept, use the following steps: concrete, practice, abstract, practice, review, test (e.g., concrete/cups and liquid, practice/using cups to solve problems, abstract/word problems with cups, practice/prepare a recipe, review, test; or concrete/cups and liquid, practice/prepare a recipe, abstract/symbols for cups, practice/word problems, review, test).

21. Have the student draw pictures to illustrate math problems.

57 Fails to correctly solve math problems requiring regrouping (borrowing and carrying)

1. Have the student solve math problems by manipulating objects to experience regrouping.

2. Assign a peer to act as a model for the student and demonstrate for the student how to correctly solve math problems that require regrouping.

3. Provide the student with many concrete experiences to help him/her learn and remember regrouping skills. Use popsicle sticks, tongue depressors, paper clips, buttons, base ten blocks, etc., to form groupings to teach regrouping.

4. Provide practice in regrouping facts using a computer software program that gives immediate feedback to the student.

5. Use daily drill activities to help the student with regrouping (e.g., written problems, flash cards, etc.).

6. Find opportunities for the student to apply regrouping to real-life situations (e.g., getting change in the cafeteria, figuring how much items will cost when added together while shopping, etc.).

7. Develop a regrouping reference for the student to use at his/her desk when solving math problems which require regrouping.

8. Have the student independently solve half of his/her math problems each day; allow the use of a calculator as reinforcement to complete the other half of the math assignment.

9. Provide the student with opportunities for tutoring from peers or teacher. Allow the student to tutor others when he/she has mastered a concept.

10. Make certain that the language used to communicate with the student about regrouping is consistent (e.g., ''borrow,'' ''carry,'' etc.).

11. Make certain the student understands number concepts and the relationship of number symbols to numbers of objects before requiring him/her to solve math problems requiring regrouping.

12. Make certain the student knows the concepts of *more than, less than, equal,* and *zero.* The use of tangible objects will facilitate the learning process.

13. Have the student practice the concept of regrouping by ''borrowing'' and ''carrying'' from objects in columns set up like math problems.

14. Provide the student with shorter math tasks, but more of them throughout the day (e.g., four assignments of five problems each rather than one assignment of twenty problems).

15. Work the first problem or two of the math assignment with the student in order to make certain that he/she understands directions and the operation necessary to solve the problem.

16. Have the student talk through math problems as he/she solves them in order to identify errors the student is making.

17. Require the student to check subtraction problems by adding (i.e., the difference plus the subtrahend equals the minuend). Reinforce the student for each error he/she corrects.

18. Have the student play games using colored chips, assigning values to each color to learn that one ten chip is equal to ten one chips.

19. Require the student to check addition problems by subtracting.

20. Have the student raise his/her hand after completing several problems in order for the teacher to check and reinforce his/her work before continuing.

21. Provide the student with learning experiences in grouping tangible objects into groups of ones, tens, hundreds, etc.

22. Have the student solve money math problems using pennies and dimes to learn the concept of regrouping and borrowing.

23. Have the student practice the concept of "borrowing" and "carrying" from graphic depictions of sets.

24. Have the student use Cuisenaire rods when solving "borrowing" and "carrying" math problems.

58 Works math problems from left to right instead of right to left

1. Have a peer tutor work with the student each day on working math problems from right to left.

2. Develop a math reference sheet for the student to keep at his/her desk (e.g., steps used in doing addition problems, subtraction problems, multiplication problems, division problems).

3. Have the student check his/her math assignments using a calculator.

4. Use large colored arrows to indicate where the student begins to work math problems (e.g., right to left).

5. Work the first problems for the student as he/she watches in order to provide a demonstration and an example.

6. Put the student's math problems on graph paper or vertically lined paper to emphasize columns, with directions to begin each problem at the right.

7. Make certain the student has mastered place value concepts and understands that columns to the left are higher values than those to the right.

8. Require the student to solve math problems by place value (e.g., begin with the ones column, then the tens column, hundreds column, etc.).

9. Write the place value above each math problem in order to remind the student to begin with the ones column to solve the problems.

10. Have the student use a calculator to solve math problems.

11. Display a large poster-board sign or use the chalkboard to create a message that indicates reading begins to the left and math problems begin to the right (e.g., READING BEGINS ON THE LEFT. MATH BEGINS ON THE RIGHT.).

12. Make certain the student understands place value to the point that he/she can explain the concept of the ones column, the tens column, etc.

13. Require the student to work each math problem using a bookmark/strip of paper to cover all columns except the one on the right and move the marker to the left as he/she moves from the ones column to the tens columns to the hundreds column, etc.

14. Use a marker to highlight the ones column to show the student where to begin to work math problems.

15. Provide the student practice in solving math problems on the computer, which will automatically solve problems right to left.

16. Have the student verbally explain steps to the teacher for solving a math problem in order to check the student's thinking processes.

17. Model proper right-to-left solving of math problems on the chalkboard or overhead projector before the student begins a new assignment.

18. Reinforce proper right-to-left problem solving through the use of math games.

19. Pair the student with another student to solve math problems on the chalkboard.

1. Reduce the emphasis on competition. Competitive activities may cause the student to hurry and fail to follow necessary steps in math problems.

2. Make certain the student recognizes all math operation symbols (e.g., +, -, ×, ÷).

3. Use written reminders (e.g., add, subtract, multiply, divide) by math problems to indicate which step is to be done. Gradually reduce the use of reminders as the student demonstrates success.

4. Put all math problems involving the same steps on a single line, on a separate sheet of paper, etc.

5. Make the math operation symbols next to the problems extra large in order that the student will be more likely to observe the symbols.

6. Color code math operation symbols next to math problems in order that the student will be more likely to observe the symbols.

7. Work the first problem or two of a math assignment for the student in order that he/she knows which steps to use.

8. Use a separate piece of paper for each type of math problem, gradually introducing different types of problems on the same page.

9. Provide the student with a list of steps necessary for the problems he/she is attempting to solve. Have the student keep a list at his/her desk for a reference while solving math problems.

10. List the steps in solving math problems on the chalkboard, bulletin board, etc.

11. Have a peer tutor work with the student while he/she learns to follow the steps in math problems.

12. Have the student check his/her answers to math problems on a calculator.

13. Have the student act as a peer tutor for another student who is learning new math concepts. Explaining steps in basic math problems will help the student cement his/her own skills.

14. Have the student equate math problems to real-life situations in order that he/she will better understand the steps involved in solving the problem (e.g., 4 × 25 is the same as 4 baskets of apples with 25 apples in each basket. How many apples do you have?).

15. Be certain to assign the student math problems requiring the same operation to make it easier for the student to follow steps in solving the problems. More than one operation may be required in an assignment as the student demonstrates success.

16. Highlight the math symbol for each math problem using a highlight marker.

17. Have the student raise his/her hand after completing several problems in order for the teacher to check and reinforce his/her work before continuing.

18. Use large colored arrows to indicate where the student should begin to work problems.

19. Have the student verbally explain steps to the teacher for solving a math problem in order to check proper sequence of steps.

20. Model proper sequence of steps when solving math problems on the chalkboard or overhead projector before the student begins a new assignment.

21. Pair the student with another student to solve math problems on the chalkboard, reinforcing the proper sequence of steps.

22. Provide the student with computer software programs that reinforce the proper sequence of steps in solving math problems.

23. Use visual cues (e.g., stop signs or red dots) on paper when the student must change operations in a multi-step math problem.

24. Before the student solves any math problems, have him/her circle each math problem's operation symbol.

25. Before the student solves any math word problems, have him/her write the name of the operation beside each word problem. Check the student's choice of operations before he/she begins to solve the problems.

60 Fails to correctly solve math problems involving fractions or decimals

1. Make certain the student understands that 8/8 equals a whole, 10/10 equals a whole, etc.

2. Make certain the student understands the concept of regrouping (e.g., changing mixed numerals into improper fractions, etc.).

3. Identify a peer to work with the student on problems involving fractions or decimals.

4. Have the student solve math problems involving fractions and decimals using computer software.

5. Have the student solve math problems involving fractions by using tangible objects (e.g., pennies which are one-tenth of a dime, inch cubes which are one-twelfth of a foot, etc.).

6. Provide the student with many concrete experiences to help him/her learn to use fractions (e.g., cutting pie-shaped pieces, measuring 1/2 cup, weighing 1/4 pound, etc.).

7. Make certain the student understands number concepts and the relationships of number symbols to numbers of objects before requiring him/her to solve math problems involving fractions.

8. Provide the student with enjoyable math activities involving fractions which he/she can perform for drill and practice either alone or with a peer (e.g., computer games, math games, manipulatives).

9. Work the first few problems of the math assignment with the student in order to make certain that he/she understand directions and the operation necessary to solve the problems.

10. Cut pieces of paper into equal numbers (e.g., fourths, sixths, tenths, etc.); have the student add fractions together, subtract fractions, etc.

11. For math problems involving fractions with unlike denominators, have the student use a tangible object such as a ruler to help him/her solve the problem (e.g., compare 3/4 to 7/8).

12. Have the student solve fraction problems by using real-life measurement such as ounces, inches, pounds, etc., to determine weight, length, volume, etc.

13. When the student is solving fraction problems, provide the student with manipulatives which represent the fractions involved.

14. Provide the student with paper to solve decimal problems which has blank boxes and decimal points in order to help guide the student to proper placement of decimal numbers.

15. Have the student solve money problems to practice decimal problems.

16. Have the student solve math problems involving decimals by using tangible objects (e.g., two dollar bills and one fifty cent piece equals $2.50, etc.).

17. Provide the student with many concrete experiences to help him/her learn to use decimals (e.g., use money, determine mileage (5.2 miles to school), etc.).

18. Have the student use a calculator when learning to solve problems involving decimals.

19. Provide the student with enjoyable math activities involving decimals which he/she can perform for drill and practice either alone or with a peer (e.g., computer games, math games, manipulatives).

20. Provide the student with a daily shopping list of items with a corresponding list of the cost of each item (each involving a decimal point). Have the student determine the cost of his/her purchase.

21. Bring a selection of menus to the classroom to have the student select items for a meal and compute the cost of the items (each involving a decimal point).

22. Have the student use a newspaper or catalog to make a list of things advertised which he/she would like to purchase. Have the student determine the total cost of the items selected using decimals.

23. Have the student earn a hypothetical income and engage in money-related math problems using decimals (e.g., taxes, social security, savings, rent, food, clothing, auto payments, recreation, etc.). The degree of difficulty of the problems is matched to the student's ability level.

1. Have the student use a calculator to reinforce learning to solve problems involving money. Have the student solve several money problems each day using the calculator.

2. Provide practice of money problems using a computer with software programs that give immediate feedback to the student.

3. Use real-life situations for the student to practice money problems (e.g., paying for lunch in the cafeteria line, making purchases from book clubs, purchasing a soft drink, etc.).

4. Use actual coins in teaching the student coin values; counting by ones, fives, tens, etc.; matching combinations of coins; etc.

5. Make certain the student recognizes all coins (e.g., penny, nickel, dime, quarter, half-dollar).

6. Make certain the student recognizes common denominations of paper money (e.g., one-dollar bill, five-dollar bill, ten-dollar bill, twenty-dollar bill, fifty-dollar bill, etc.).

7. Have a peer work with the student every day practicing coin values, paper money values, combinations, etc.

8. Have the student match equal values of coins (e.g., two nickels equal a dime, two dimes and a nickel equal a quarter, five nickels equal a quarter, etc.).

9. Make certain the student understands all math operation concepts involved in using money (e.g., addition, subtraction, multiplication, division, decimals, etc.).

10. Have the student match equal values of bills (e.g., five one-dollar bills equal a five-dollar bill, two five-dollar bills equal a ten-dollar bill, etc.).

11. Make certain the student can solve the necessary math problems involved in the use of money (i.e., the student can solve math problems of the same difficulty as those involving money).

12. Make certain the student can count by pennies, nickels, dimes, quarters, half-dollars.

13. Have the student use actual money to simulate transactions in the classroom (e.g., purchasing lunch, groceries, snacks, clothing, etc.). Have the student practice acting as both a customer and a clerk.

14. Provide the student with math word problems involving the use of money, making certain the appropriate operation is clearly stated.

15. Provide the student with a daily shopping list of items with a corresponding list of the cost of each item. Have the student determine the cost of his/her purchase.

16. Bring a selection of menus to the classroom to have the student select items for a meal and compute the cost of the items.

17. Have the student use a newspaper or catalog to make a list of things advertised which he/she would like to purchase. Have the student determine the total cost of the items selected.

18. Have the student earn a hypothetical income and engage in money-related math problems (e.g., taxes, social security, savings, rent, food, clothing, auto payments, recreation, etc.). The degree of difficulty of the problems is matched to the student's ability level.

19. Have the student talk through money math problems as he/she solves them in order to identify errors.

20. Make certain the student can count by ones, fives, tens, twenties.

62 Fails to correctly solve problems using measurement

1. Discuss and provide the student with a list of words/phrases which usually indicate measurement problems (e.g., pounds, inches, millimeter, kilogram, etc.).

2. Assign a peer to act as a model for the student to demonstrate how to solve measurement problems.

3. Find opportunities for the student to apply measurement facts to real-life situations (e.g., cooking, measuring the lengths of objects, etc.).

4. Develop a measurement reference sheet for the student to use at his/her desk when solving math problems.

5. Provide the student with enjoyable measurement activities during free time in the classroom (e.g., computer games, math games, etc.).

6. Make certain that the language used to communicate with the student about measurement is consistent (e.g., meters, grams, etc.).

7. Make certain the student has mastery of math concepts at each level before introducing a new skill.

8. Work the first problem or two of the math assignment with the student in order to make certain that he/she understands directions and the operation necessary to solve the problem.

9. Have the student practice basic measurement concepts (e.g., pound, ounce, inch, foot, etc.) using everyday measurement devices in the environment (e.g., scale, measuring cup, ruler, etc.).

10. Have the student practice measuring items in the environment to find their length, weight, etc.

11. Make certain the student knows the basic concepts of fractions before requiring him/her to solve problems involving fractional measurement (e.g., 1/4 inch, 1 1/2 feet, etc.).

12. Assign the student measurement problems that he/she will want to be able to perform successfully (e.g., following a cooking recipe, building a model, etc.).

13. Have the student practice using smaller units of measurement to create larger units of measurement (e.g., twelve inches to make one foot, three feet to make one yard, eight ounces to make one cup, four cups to make one quart, etc.).

14. Have the student begin solving problems using measurement which require same and whole units (e.g., 10 pounds minus 8 pounds, 24 inches plus 12 inches, etc.). Introduce fractions and mixed units (e.g., pounds and ounces, etc.) only after the student has demonstrated success with same and whole units.

15. Have the student use a calculator to solve measurement problems and check the accuracy of problems he/she has worked.

16. Have the student use computer software programs to practice measurement skills.

17. Have the student solve beginning measurement problems using measurement devices before solving the problems on paper (e.g., 5 inches plus 4 inches using a ruler, 3 liquid ounces plus 5 liquid ounces using a measuring cup, etc.).

63 Fails to use capitalization correctly when writing

1. Make certain the student receives instruction in the rules of capitalization (e.g., first word of a sentence, the pronoun I, proper names, cities, states, streets, months, days of the week, dates, holidays, titles of movies, books, newspapers, magazines, etc.).

2. Make certain the student knows how to make all the capital letters of the alphabet.

3. Highlight or underline all the capitalized letters in a passage or paragraph and have the student explain why each is capitalized.

4. Have the student engage in writing activities which will cause him/her to do as well as possible in capitalization and other writing skills (e.g., writing letters to a friend, rock star, famous athlete, etc.).

5. Emphasize one rule of capitalization until the student masters that rule before moving on to another rule (e.g., proper names, cities, states, streets, etc.).

6. Provide the student with lists of words and have him/her indicate which should be capitalized (e.g., water, new york, mississippi, etc.).

7. Have the student practice writing words which are always capitalized (e.g., countries, bodies of water, nationalities, languages, capitols, days of the week, months of the year, etc.).

8. Make certain the student proofreads his/her work for correct capitalization. Reinforce the student for each correction made in capitalization.

9. After checking the student's work, require him/her to make all necessary corrections in capitalization.

10. Give the student a series of sentences representing all the capitalization rules. Have the student identify the rules for each capitalization. Remove each sentence from the assignment when the student can explain the rules for the capitalization in the sentence.

11. Make certain the student has a list of rules for capitalization at his/her desk to use as a reference.

12. Provide the student with a list of examples of capitalization (e.g., proper names, cities, streets, holidays, etc.) that the student keeps at his/her desk to refer to when writing.

13. Have the student practice correct capitalization by providing the student with several sentences with errors on the chalkboard or overhead projector. The student is then expected to correct the capitalization errors and discuss with the teacher.

14. Model appropriate capitalization of sentences when assigning creative writing activities. This could be done on the chalkboard, an overhead projector or in chart form.

15. Review with the student common capitalization rules before starting a creative writing activity.

16. Provide the student with computer software that provides practice and reinforcement in capitalizing words.

64 Fails to punctuate correctly when writing

1. Reduce the emphasis on competition. Competitive activities may cause the student to hurry and make errors in punctuation.

2. Give the student sentences requiring him/her to fill in specific punctuation he/she is learning to use (e.g., periods, commas, question marks, etc.).

3. Have the student practice using one form of punctuation at a time before going on to another (e.g., period, question mark, etc.).

4. Highlight or underline punctuation in passages from the student's reading assignment. Have the student explain why each form of punctuation is used.

5. Require the student to proofread all written work for correct punctuation. Reinforce the student for each correction he/she makes on punctuation.

6. Have the student keep a list of basic rules of punctuation at his/her desk to use as a reference when writing (e.g., use a period at the end of a sentence, etc.).

7. Make certain the student receives instruction in the rules of punctuation (e.g., periods belong at the end of sentences, question marks are used when a question is asked, etc.).

8. Make certain the student knows what all punctuation marks look like and their uses.

9. After checking the student's work, require him/her to make all necessary corrections in punctuation.

10. Have the student engage in writing activities which will cause him/her to do as well as possible on punctuation and other writing skills (e.g., writing letters to a friend, rock star, famous athlete, etc.).

11. Give the student a series of sentences representing all the punctuation rules. Have the student identify the rules for each punctuation. Remove each sentence from the assignment when the student can explain the rules for punctuation in the sentence.

12. Provide the student with a list of examples of the forms of punctuation he/she is expected to use (e.g., periods, commas, question marks, exclamation points, etc.). The student keeps the examples at his/her desk and refers to them when writing.

13. Have the student practice correct punctuation by providing the student with several sentences with errors on the chalkboard. The student is then expected to correct the punctuation errors and discuss with the teacher.

14. Provide the student with computer software which provides practice and reinforcement in punctuating sentences and other creative writing assignments (e.g., addresses, letters, etc.).

15. Review with the student common punctuation rules before starting a creative writing activity.

16. Model appropriate punctuation through charts and overheads for student reference during all creative writing activities.

65 Does not use appropriate subject-verb agreement when writing

1. Require the student to proofread his/her written work for subject-verb agreement. Reinforce the student for correcting all errors.

2. Have the student complete written worksheets on which he/she must supply the correct verb form to go with specific subjects (e.g., "He _____ the dishes.").

3. Have the student choose the correct verb when given choices on "fill-in-the-blank" worksheets (e.g., "They _____(have, has) a new dog.").

4. Give the student specific verb forms and have him/her supply appropriate subjects to go with each (e.g., "_____ runs.").

5. Have the student make up sentences with given verbs and subjects.

6. Have the student help correct other students' written work by checking subject-verb agreement and correcting the assignment.

7. Give the student a series of sentences with both incorrect and correct usage of verbs and ask the student to identify which are correct and incorrect.

8. Have the student find examples of correct subject-verb agreement in his/her favorite books or magazines.

9. Identify the most common errors the student makes in subject-verb agreement. Have the student spend time each day writing one or more of these subject-verb combinations in correct form.

10. Make a list of the correct forms of subject-verbs the student has difficulty writing correctly. Have the student keep the list at his/her desk for a reference when writing.

11. Reduce the emphasis on competition. Competitive activities may cause the student to hurry and make errors in subject-verb agreement.

12. Make certain the student receives instruction in subject-verb agreement for those subject-verb combinations he/she commonly has difficulty writing correctly.

13. Correct the student each time he/she uses subject-verb agreement incorrectly when speaking.

14. Make certain the student knows that different forms of verbs go with different subjects and that correct subject-verb agreement requires the appropriate verb form. Have the student practice matching verb forms to lists of subjects.

15. Have the student read the written work of peers in which subject-verb agreement is used correctly.

16. Highlight or underline subject-verb agreements in the student's reading in order to call attention to the appropriate combinations.

17. After checking the student's written work, make certain he/she makes all necessary corrections in subject-verb agreement.

18. Model appropriate subject-verb agreement when speaking in order that the student learns appropriate subject-verb agreement through verbal channels.

19. Provide the student with computer software programs that give practice and reinforcement in subject-verb agreement.

20. Provide a review of standard subject-verb agreement rules through a chart posted in the classroom (e.g., cows run, a cow runs, etc.).

21. Have the student practice correct subject-verb agreement by providing the student with several sentences with errors on the chalkboard or overhead. The student is then expected to correct the subject-verb errors and discuss with the teacher.

66 Does not compose complete sentences or express complete thoughts when writing

1. Reduce the emphasis on competition. Competitive activities may cause the student to hurry and fail to write in complete sentences.

2. Identify the qualities a good writer possesses (e.g., writing in complete sentences or thoughts, using correct vocabulary, etc.) and have the student evaluate himself/herself on each characteristic. Set a goal for improvement in only one or two areas at a time.

3. Have the student identify who he/she thinks is a good writer and why.

4. Have a peer act as a model for writing in complete sentences or thoughts. Assign students to work together, perform assignments together, etc.

5. Be certain to act as a model for the student to imitate writing in complete sentences or thoughts.

6. Require the student to proofread all written work and reinforce him/her for completing sentences or thoughts.

7. Give the student a series of written phrases and have him/her indicate which ones express a complete thought.

8. Have the student correct a series of phrases by making each a complete sentence.

9. After reading his/her written work, have the student explain why specific sentences do not express complete thoughts.

10. Give the student a subject and have him/her write as many complete sentences about it as possible.

11. Make groups of cards containing subjects, verbs, adjectives, etc. Have the student combine the cards in various ways to construct complete sentences.

12. Give the student several short sentences and have him/her combine them in order to make one longer complete sentence (e.g., "The dog is big. The dog is brown. The dog is mine." becomes "The big, brown dog is mine.").

13. Give the student a list of conjunction words (e.g., therefore, although, because, etc.) and have him/her make sentences using each word.

14. Make certain the student understands that a complete sentence has to express a complete thought about a subject and what that subject is or does.

15. Have the student write a daily log, expressing his/her thoughts in complete sentences.

16. Have the student write letters to friends, relatives, etc., in order to create additional ways he/she can practice writing complete sentences and thoughts.

17. Encourage the student to read his/her written work aloud in order to help him/her identify incomplete sentences and thoughts.

18. Give the student a group of related words (e.g., *author, read, love, best-seller*, etc.) and have him/her make up a paragraph including all the words.

19. Have a peer read the student's written work aloud in order to help him/her identify incomplete sentences.

20. Give the student a note card to keep at his/her desk to serve as a reminder that all sentences must have a subject and a verb.

21. Provide the student with examples of subjects and verbs on a classroom chart.

22. Teach the student to proofread each sentence in isolation to check for a complete thought.

67 Fails to correctly organize writing activities

1. Have the student practice organizational skills in writing activities by engaging in writing activities designed to cause him/her to want to be successful (e.g., writing a letter to a friend, rock star, famous athlete, etc.).

2. Have the student write a weekly account of the previous week, past weekend, etc., with primary attention given to organization (e.g., sequencing events, developing a paragraph, using correct word order, etc.).

3. Require the student to proofread all written work. Reinforce all corrections in organization.

4. Have the student create his/her own stories about topics which interest him/her. The student is more likely to try to be successful if he/she is writing about something of interest.

5. Have the student read his/her own written work aloud to help him/her identify errors in organization.

6. Make certain the student knows that paragraphs, essays, etc., need an introduction, a body where information is contained, and a conclusion or ending.

7. Have the student arrange a series of statements on a topic in an appropriate order so that they make sense in a paragraph.

8. Teach outlining principles to the student so he/she understands the difference between main ideas and supporting details.

9. Help the student "brainstorm" ideas about a topic and then show him/her how to put these ideas into outline form, combining some ideas and discarding others.

10. Provide the student with a paragraph in which one statement does not belong. Have the student find the inappropriate statement.

11. Have the student write step-by-step directions (e.g., steps in making a cake) so he/she can practice sequencing events.

12. Give the student a group of related words (e.g., *author, read, love, best-seller*, etc.) and have him/her make up an appropriately organized paragraph including each word.

13. Using a written essay that the student has not seen, cut the paragraphs apart and ask him/her to reconstruct the essay by putting the paragraphs in the appropriate order.

14. Reduce the emphasis on competition. Competitive activities may cause the student to hurry and fail to correctly organize his/her writing activities.

15. Reduce distracting stimuli by placing the student in a study carrel or "office" when engaged in writing activities. This is used as a means of reducing distracting stimuli and not as a form of punishment.

16. Make certain the student is not interrupted or hurried when engaging in writing activities.

17. Have the student read sentences, paragraphs, stories, etc., written by peers who demonstrate good organizational skills in writing.

18. When correcting the student's organizational skills in writing, be certain to provide evaluative feedback which is designed to be instructional (e.g., help the student rewrite for better organization, rewrite passages for the student, etc.).

19. Have the student develop organizational skills in writing simple sentences. Gradually increase the required complexity of sentence structure and move on to paragraphs, short stories, etc., as the student demonstrates success.

20. Have the student develop an outline or "skeleton" of what he/she is going to write. From the outline the student can then practice organizational skills in writing.

21. Have the student read a short story and then list the events of the story. From that list, have the student construct a paragraph using the correct sequence of events.

22. Give the student several short sentences and have him/her combine them in order to make one longer complete sentences (e.g., "The dog is big. The dog is brown. The dog is mine." becomes "The big, brown dog is mine.").

23. Have the student begin to practice organizational writing skills by writing simple sentences with subjects and verbs. Have the student then expound the sentences by adding adjectives, adverbs and prepositional phrases.

24. Have the student practice writing paragraphs according to "Who, What, Where, When, How, and Why."

25. Have the student begin to practice organizational writing skills by writing simple sentences. The student should then write related simple sentences to form paragraphs. This practice should be used to form new paragraphs and more extensive writing activities.

68 Fails to use spelling rules

1. Reduce the emphasis on competition. Competitive activities may cause the student to hurry and make mistakes.

2. Have a peer spend time each day with the student practicing the use of spelling rules when writing words, sentences, etc.

3. Have the student practice using spelling rules in words, sentences, etc., which he/she writes every day.

4. Teach spelling rules integrated with the total language arts program (e.g., activities, methods, and materials are related to the teaching of spelling, reading, and language as a whole rather than in parts).

5. Require the student to use a dictionary to find the correct spelling of any word he/she cannot spell correctly. The emphasis in this situation becomes spelling accurately rather than memorizing spelling words.

6. Have the student practice spelling rules in a meaningful manner which will cause him/her to want to be successful (e.g., writing a letter to a friend, rock star, famous athlete, etc.).

7. Make certain the student knows why he/she is learning spelling rules (e.g., provide the student with a concrete example of how each word can be used in his/her life).

8. Have the student identify a list of spelling words (e.g., 5, 10, or 15) each week from an area of interest. Have the student learn to spell these words using the spelling rules.

9. Make certain the student has had adequate practice using spelling rules in writing words, sentences, etc.

10. Make certain the student has adequate time to perform written assignments in order that he/she will be more likely to use spelling rules.

11. Make certain the student is not being required to learn too many spelling words at one time.

12. Make certain the student learns to use spelling rules to spell words correctly rather than simply memorizing the spelling of words for testing purposes (e.g., dropping the *e* when adding *ing*, etc.).

13. Have the student keep a commercial dictionary of "most misspelled words" at his/her desk and require him/her to check the spelling of all words he/she is not certain are spelled correctly.

14. Have the student practice any one spelling rule consistently until that rule is mastered (e.g., dropping the *e* when adding *ing*, etc.). When one rule is mastered, a new one is introduced.

15. Require the student to proofread his/her written assignments using spelling rules. Reinforce the student for each correction he/she makes when using spelling rules.

16. Develop a list of spelling rules. Have the student keep the list of spelling rules at his/her desk and require the student to refer to the rules when writing words, sentences, etc.

17. Require the student to verbally explain how he/she spells words using spelling rules (e.g., dropping the *e* when adding *ing*, etc.).

18. Require the student to practice those basic spelling rules which he/she uses on a daily basis.

19. Provide computer software programs which give practice and reinforcement for correctly spelling words.

20. Provide the student with commercial or teacher-made games which provide practice in using spelling rules.

21. Pair the student with a peer to proofread each other's work.

22. Post a chart with a list of spelling rules taught in order that the student can refer to it when completing written assignments.

23. Have a list of word endings (e.g., *-ed, -ing, -ly, -er*, etc.) and sample words attached to the student's desk for use as a reference when writing.

24. Use wall charts showing word endings (e.g., *-ed, -ing, -ly, -er*, etc.) and sample words for the student to use as a reference when writing.

25. Have the student spend time each day practicing the use of one word ending (e.g., *-ed*). When the student demonstrates mastery of a word ending, he/she begins practicing a new one.

26. Highlight or underline word endings (e.g., *-ed, -ing, -ly, -er*, etc.) in the student's reading assignments in order to call attention to the appropriate use of word endings.

27. Have the student keep a copy of the rules for word endings at his/her desk.

28. Provide the student with a list of examples of words which represent the spelling rules that the student keeps at his/her desk for reference (e.g., "hoping" represents dropping the *e* when adding *ing*, "hopping" represents doubling the consonant when adding *ing*, etc.).

29. Post a chart in the classroom with a list of examples of words which represent the spelling rules that the student can refer to when completing written assignments (e.g., "hoping" represents dropping the *e* when adding *ing*, "hopping" represents doubling the consonant when adding *ing*, etc.).

30. Have the student start a personal dictionary of misspelled words at his/her desk and require him/her to check the spelling of all words he/she is not certain are spelled correctly.

69 Omits, substitutes, adds, or rearranges letters or sound units when spelling words

1. Reduce the emphasis on competition. Competitive activities may cause the student to hurry and misspell words.

2. Give the student fewer words to learn to spell at any one time, spending more time on each word until the student can spell it correctly.

3. Have a peer spend time each day with the student engaged in drill activities on spelling words.

4. Identify those words the student misspells by omitting, substituting, adding, or rearranging letters or sound units. Have the student practice spelling the words correctly in sentences he/she writes each day.

5. Require the student to use the dictionary to find the correct spelling of any word he/she cannot spell correctly. The emphasis in this situation becomes spelling accurately rather than memorizing spelling words.

6. Have the student practice his/her spelling in a meaningful manner which would cause him/her to want to be successful (e.g., writing a letter to a friend, rock star, famous athlete, etc.).

7. Make certain the student knows why he/she needs to spell words correctly (e.g., provide the student with a concrete example of how each word can be used in his/her life).

8. Have the student identify a list of words (e.g., 5, 10, or 15) each week from an area of interest. If the student is interested in cars, he/she can identify words from automotive magazines, advertisements, etc.

9. Have the student keep a commercial dictionary of "most misspelled words" at his/her desk and require him/her to check the spelling of all words he/she is not certain are spelled correctly.

10. Make certain the student is not being required to learn too many words at one time.

11. Make certain that the student's spelling words are those which he/she sees on a routine basis rather than infrequently, in order to assure correct spelling and use of the words.

12. Make a list of letters or sound units the student omits, substitutes, adds, or rearranges. Have the student practice spelling words using the letters or sound units correctly.

13. Make a list of the words the student misspells by omitting, substituting, adding, or rearranging letters or sound units. Have the student practice spelling the words correctly, removing each word from the list as the student demonstrates mastery.

14. Highlight or underline in the student's reading assignments those letters or sound units that the student omits, substitutes, adds, or rearranges, in order to direct the student's attention to the correct spelling of words.

15. Have the student proofread his/her written work for omissions, substitutions, additions, or rearranged letters or sound units. Reinforce the student for each correction he/she makes.

16. Make certain the student "hears" correctly those letters or sound units he/she omits, substitutes, adds, or rearranges when spelling words. Have the student say the words aloud to determine if the student is aware of the letters or sound units in the words.

17. Identify those words the student misspells by omitting, substituting, adding, or rearranging letters or sound units. Provide personalized computer software which will allow the student to practice his/her personal word list.

18. Provide opportunities for the student to read often in order that the student sees in print those words he/she needs to learn to spell.

19. Identify those words the student misspells by omitting, substituting, adding, or rearranging letters or sound units. Have the student start and frequently update a personalized dictionary to use as a reference.

20. Provide commercial or teacher-made games which provide practice in spelling. The student should have a personalized list of words for this practice.

Reminder: If the student continually omits, substitutes, adds, or rearranges letters or sound units when spelling words, the educator may wish to pursue formal referral and further assessment.

70 Has difficulty spelling words that do not follow the spelling rules

1. Give the student fewer words to learn to spell at any one time, spending more time on each word until the student can spell it correctly.

2. Have a peer spend time each day with the student practicing spelling words which do not follow the spelling rules.

3. Have the student write his/her spelling words in different locations throughout the classroom as he/she is learning them (e.g., on the chalkboard, on transparencies, on a posted list at his/her desk, etc.).

4. Require the student to use a dictionary to find the correct spelling of any words he/she cannot spell correctly. The emphasis in this situation becomes spelling accurately rather than memorizing spelling words.

5. Have the student identify a list of spelling words (e.g., 5, 10, or 15) each week from an area of interest. These words become the student's spelling words for the week.

6. Make certain the student has adequate time to perform written assignments in order that he/she will be more likely to spell words correctly.

7. Have the student keep a commercial dictionary of "most misspelled words" at his/her desk and require him/her to check the spelling of all words he/she is not certain are spelled correctly.

8. Require the student to proofread his/her written assignments for spelling errors. Reinforce the student for each correction he/she makes.

9. Identify the most common words the student uses which do not follow spelling rules. Have the student learn to spell these words as a sight word vocabulary.

10. Develop a spelling list of words the student uses which do not follow the spelling rules. Add new words to the list as the student demonstrates mastery of any of the words.

11. Make certain the student does not have too many words to learn to spell at one time.

12. Make a list of the words the student most commonly misspells. Keep a copy of the list of correctly spelled words at his/her desk to use as a reference when writing.

13. Have the student use his/her current spelling words in a meaningful manner which would cause him/her to want to be successful (e.g., writing a letter to a friend, rock star, famous athlete, etc.).

14. Make certain the student "hears" the sounds in the words he/she misspells. Have the student say the words aloud to determine if the student is aware of the letters or sound units in the words.

15. Provide opportunities for the student to read often in order that the student sees in print those words he/she needs to learn to spell.

16. Provide computer software that provides practice and reinforcement in spelling words correctly.

17. Provide commercial or teacher-made games which give practice in spelling words which do not follow the spelling rules.

18. Make a list of frequently seen words which do not follow spelling rules for the student to keep at his/her desk.

19. Teach spelling integrated with the total language arts program (e.g., activities, methods, and materials are related to the teaching of reading and language as a whole rather than in parts).

20. Try various activities to help strengthen and reinforce the phonetic spelling of words (e.g., writing his/her own story, sentences, etc.).

21. Make certain the student knows the sounds that letters make. Have the student practice making letter sounds as he/she sees the letters on flash cards.

22. Have the student write sentences, paragraphs, or a story each day about a favorite subject. Encourage the student to use available references (e.g., dictionary, lists of words, etc.) to insure proper spelling.

71 Spells words correctly in one context but not in another

1. Reduce the emphasis on competition. Competitive activities may cause the student to hurry and make mistakes in spelling.

2. Give the student fewer words to learn to spell at any one time, spending more time on each word until the student can spell it correctly.

3. Have the student use his/her spelling words in different sentences he/she writes each day.

4. Write sentences, paragraphs, etc., for the student to read which repeat the student's spelling words throughout the written material.

5. Have a list of the student's current spelling words taped on his/her desk with the requirement that they be practiced whenever the student has time. Reinforce the student for practicing the writing of the spelling words within sentences and paragraphs.

6. Teach spelling integrated with the total language arts program (e.g., activities, methods, and materials are related to the teaching of reading and language as a whole rather than in parts).

7. Require the student to use the dictionary to find the correct spelling of any word he/she cannot spell correctly. The emphasis in this situation becomes spelling accurately rather than memorizing spelling words.

8. Have the student use his/her current spelling words in a meaningful manner which would cause him/her to want to be successful (e.g., writing a letter to a friend, rock star, famous athlete, etc.).

9. Make certain the student knows why he/she is learning each spelling word (e.g., provide the student with a concrete example of how each word can be used in his/her life).

10. Make certain the student has had adequate practice in writing the spelling words (e.g., drill activities, sentence activities, etc.).

11. Have the student identify a list of spelling words (e.g., 5, 10, or 15) each week from an area of interest. If the student is interested in cars, he/she can identify words from automotive magazines, advertisements, etc.

12. Try various activities to help strengthen and reinforce the visual memory of the spelling words (e.g., flash cards, word lists on the chalkboard, a list on the student's desk, etc.).

13. Make certain the student has adequate time to perform written assignments.

14. Have the student maintain a folder of all of his/her spelling words. Require the student to refer to the list when he/she is engaged in writing activities in order to check spelling.

15. Make certain the student learns to "use" spelling words rather than simply memorizing the spelling of the words for testing purposes (e.g., have the student use the words in writing activities each day).

16. Require the student to proofread all of his/her written work for spelling errors. Reinforce him/her for correcting each spelling error.

17. Have the student keep a commercial dictionary of "most misspelled words" at his/her desk and require him/her to check the spelling of all words he/she is not certain are spelled correctly.

18. Require the student to write his/her spelling words frequently over a period of time, in order to increase the student's visual memory of the spelling words.

19. Make certain that the student's spelling words are those which he/she sees on a routine basis rather than infrequently, in order to assure correct spelling and use of the words.

20. Provide opportunities for the student to read often in order that the student sees in print those words he/she needs to learn to spell.

21. Provide opportunities for the student to use computer software to write stories. He/she should then check the spelling of words with the computer's spell check.

22. Require the student to proofread his/her written work, circling any words which he/she thinks are misspelled. The student then checks with the teacher or the dictionary to correct those misspellings.

72 Requires continued drill and practice in order to learn spelling words

1. Reduce the emphasis on competition. Competitive activities may cause the student to hurry and make mistakes in spelling.

2. Give the student fewer words to learn to spell at any one time, spending more time on each word until the student can spell it correctly.

3. Have a peer spend time each day with the student engaged in drill activities on spelling words.

4. Have the student use his/her spelling words in sentences he/she writes each day.

5. Have the student highlight or underline his/her spelling words in passages from reading assignments, newspapers, magazines, etc.

6. Develop crossword puzzles which contain only the student's spelling words and have him/her complete them.

7. Write sentences, passages, paragraphs, etc., for the student to read which repeat the student's spelling words throughout the written material.

8. Have the student act as a peer tutor to teach his/her spelling words to another student.

9. Have the student write his/her spelling words in different locations throughout the classroom as he/she is learning them (e.g., on the chalkboard, on transparencies, on a posted list, at his/her desk, etc.).

10. Have the student indicate when he/she has learned one of the spelling words. As the student demonstrates he/she can spell the word, it is removed from the current spelling list.

11. Have a list of the student's current spelling words taped to his/her desk with the requirement that they be practiced whenever the student has time. Reinforce the student for practicing the writing of the spelling words.

12. Have the student review his/her spelling words each day for a short period of time rather than two or three times per week for longer periods of time.

13. Introduce words by using wall charts with visual images such as pictures for the student to associate with the letter sound.

14. Teach spelling integrated with the total language arts program (e.g., activities, methods, and materials are related to the teaching of reading and language as a whole rather than in parts).

15. Require the student to use a dictionary to find the correct spelling of any word he/she cannot spell correctly. The emphasis in this situation becomes spelling accurately rather than memorizing spelling words.

16. Have the student quiz others over his/her spelling words (e.g., teacher, aide, peers, etc.).

17. Make certain that the student's spelling instruction is on a level where success can be met. Gradually increase the degree of difficulty as the student demonstrates success.

18. Initiate a "Learn to Spell a Word a Day" program with the student.

19. Use words which are commonly found in daily surroundings for the student's spelling list (e.g., commercials, hazard signs, directions, lunch menu, etc.).

20. Make certain the student knows why he/she is learning each spelling word (e.g., provide the student with a concrete example of how each word can be used in his/her life).

21. Have the student use his/her current spelling words in a meaningful manner which would cause him/her to want to be successful (e.g., writing a letter to a friend, rock star, famous athlete, etc.).

22. Require the student to proofread all of his/her written work for spelling errors. Reinforce the student for correcting each spelling error.

23. Have the student's current spelling words listed on the chalkboard at all times.

24. Have the student identify a list of spelling words (e.g., 5, 10, or 15) each week from an area of interest. If the student is interested in cars, he/she can identify words from automotive magazines, advertisements, etc.

25. Provide the student with computer software that gives practice and reinforcement in spelling words correctly.

26. Furnish the student with commercial or teacher-made games which provide practice in spelling words.

27. Provide opportunities for the student to read often in order that the student sees in print those words which he/she needs to learn to spell.

73 Understands what is read to him/her but not what he/she reads silently

1. Make certain the student is reading material on his/her level.

2. Modify or adjust reading material to the student's ability level.

3. Outline reading material the student reads silently using words and phrases on his/her reading level.

4. Tape record difficult reading material for the student to listen to as he/she reads along.

5. Use lower grade-level texts as alternative reading material in subject areas.

6. Make a list of main points from the student's reading material, written on the student's reading level.

7. Reduce distracting stimuli in order to increase the student's ability to concentrate on what he/she is reading (e.g., place the student in the front row, provide a carrel or "office" space away from distractions, etc.). This is used as a means of reducing distracting stimuli and not as a form of punishment.

8. Provide the student a quiet place (e.g., carrel, study booth, etc.) where he/she may go to engage in reading activities.

9. Have the student verbally paraphrase material he/she has just read in order to assess his/her comprehension.

10. Teach the student to identify main points in material he/she has read in order to assess his/her comprehension.

11. Have the student outline, underline, or highlight important points in reading material.

12. Have the student take notes while he/she is reading in order to increase comprehension.

13. Have the student read progressively longer segments of reading material in order to build comprehension skills (e.g., begin with a single paragraph and progress to several paragraphs, short stories, chapters, etc.).

14. Have the student tape record what he/she reads in order to enhance comprehension by listening to the material read.

15. Teach the student to use context clues to identify words and phrases he/she does not know.

16. Write paragraphs and short stories requiring reading skills the student is currently developing. These passages should be of high interest to the student using his/her name, family members, friends, pets, and interesting experiences.

17. Have the student read high-interest signs, advertisements, notices, etc., from newspapers, magazines, movie promotions, etc., placing emphasis on comprehension skills.

18. Make certain the student is practicing comprehension skills which are directly related to high-interest reading activities (e.g., adventures, romance, mystery, athletics, etc.).

19. Underline or highlight important points before the student reads the assigned material silently.

20. Write notes and letters to the student to provide reading material which he/she will want to read for comprehension. Students may be encouraged to write each other notes and letters at a time set aside each day, once a week, etc.

21. Give the student time to read a selection more than once, emphasizing comprehension not speed.

22. Use a sight word vocabulary approach in order to teach the student key words and phrases when reading directions and instructions (e.g., key words such as *circle, underline, match,* etc.).

23. Teach the student to think about the reading selection and predict what will happen next, prior to completing the selection.

24. Teach the student to look for key words (e.g., Christopher Columbus, Spain, New World, etc.).

25. Teach the student to look for action words (e.g., sailed, discovered, founded, etc.).

26. Teach the student to look for direction words (e.g., circle, underline, choose, list, etc.).

27. Teach the student when reading to look for key words and main ideas that answer "Who, What, Where, When, How, and Why" (e.g., "Christopher Columbus sailed from Spain to discover the New World during the year 1492-.").

28. Make available for the student a learning center where a variety of information is available in content areas (e.g., the library may have a selection of films, slides, videotapes, taped lectures, etc.).

29. Have the student practice reading and following written directions in order to enhance comprehension (e.g., following a recipe, following directions to put together a model, etc.).

30. Have the student practice comprehension skills which are directly related to high-interest reading activities (e.g., adventures, romance, mystery, sports, etc.).

31. Teach the student meanings of abbreviations in order to assist in comprehending material read. (See Appendix for Selected Abbreviations and Symbols.)

32. Have the student outline reading material using the Outline Form. (See Appendix.)

33. Have the student read independently each day to practice reading skills.

34. Give the student high-interest reading material requiring him/her to answer the questions "Who, What, Where, When, How and Why" (e.g, comic books, adventure stories, etc.).

35. Teach new vocabulary words prior to having the student read the material.

36. Pair the student with a peer to summarize material read in order to answer the questions "Who, What, Where, When, How and Why."

37. Have the student answer in writing the questions "Who, What, Where, When, How and Why" using the Flash Card Study Aid. (See Appendix.)

38. When reading orally with the student, pause at various points to discuss material read up to that point. Have the student predict what will happen next before proceeding.

39. After reading a selection, have the student complete a semantic map answering the questions "Who, What, Where, When, How, and Why." (See Appendix for Mapping Form.)

40. Prior to reading a selection, familiarize the student with the general content of the story (e.g., if the selection is about elephants, brainstorm and discuss elephants to develop a point of reference).

74 Does not comprehend what he/she reads

1. Make certain the student is reading material on his/her ability level.

2. Modify or adjust the student's reading material to his/her level.

3. Outline reading material for the student using words and phrases on his/her ability level prior to reading the material.

4. Tape record difficult reading material for the student to listen to as he/she reads along.

5. Teach the student to use related learning experiences in his/her classes (e.g., filmstrips, movies, tape recordings, demonstrations, discussions, lectures, videotapes, etc.). Encourage teachers to provide alternative learning experiences for the student.

6. Arrange for a peer tutor to read with the student to develop comprehension skills.

7. Use lower grade-level texts as alternative reading material in subject areas.

8. Make a list of main points from the student's reading material, written on the student's reading level.

9. Make available for the student a learning center area where a variety of information is available for him/her in content areas (e.g., the library may have a section with films, slides, videotapes and taped lectures on such subjects as pilgrims, the Civil War, the judicial system, etc.).

10. Reduce distracting stimuli in order to increase the student's ability to concentrate on what he/she is reading (e.g., place the student in the front row, provide a carrel or "office" space away from distractions, etc.). This is used as a means of reducing distracting stimuli and not as a form of punishment.

11. Provide the student with a quiet place (e.g., carrel, study booth, etc.) where he/she may go to engage in reading activities.

12. Have the student verbally paraphrase material he/she has just read in order to assess his/her comprehension.

13. Teach the student to identify main points in material he/she has just read in order to assess his/her comprehension.

14. Have the student outline, underline, or highlight important points in reading material.

15. Provide the student with written direction-following activities in order to enhance comprehension (e.g., following a recipe, following directions to put together a model, etc.).

16. Provide the student with written one-, two-, and three-step direction-following activities (e.g., sharpen your pencil, open your text to page 121, etc.).

17. Have the student take notes while he/she is reading in order to increase comprehension.

18. Have the student read progressively longer segments of reading material in order to build comprehension skills (e.g., begin with a single paragraph and progress to several paragraphs, a chapter, a short story, a novel, etc.).

19. Have the student tape record what he/she reads in order to enhance comprehension by listening to the material read.

20. Teach the student to use context clues to identify words and phrases he/she does not know.

21. Underline or highlight important points before the student reads the assigned material silently.

22. Have the student read a selection more than once, emphasizing comprehension rather than speed.

23. Use reading series material with high interest and low vocabulary for the older student.

24. Teach the student to think about the reading selection and predict what will happen prior to reading the selection.

25. Teach the student to look for key words (e.g., Christopher Columbus, Spain, New World, etc.).

26. Teach the student to look for action words (e.g., sailed, discovered, founded).

27. Teach the student to look for direction words (e.g., circle, underline, choose, list, etc.).

28. Teach the student to look for the key words and main ideas when reading that answer "Who, What, Where, When, How, and Why" (e.g., "Christopher Columbus sailed from Spain to discover the New World during the year 1492.").

29. Teach the student meanings of abbreviations in order to assist in comprehending material read. (See Appendix for Selected Abbreviations and Symbols.)

30. Prior to reading a selection, familiarize the student with the general content of the story (e.g., when reading a selection about birds, have the students brainstorm and discuss birds to develop a point of reference).

31. Teach the student to look for story elements when reading a selection (e.g., setting, characters, plot, ending). (See Appendix for Fiction Frame.)

32. After reading a selection, have the student complete a semantic map answering the questions "Who, What, Where, When, How, and Why." (See Appendix for Mapping Form.)

33. Have the student outline reading material using the Outline Form. (See Appendix.)

34. Have the student read independently each day to practice reading skills.

35. Give the student high-interest reading material requiring him/her to answer the questions "Who, What, Where, When, How and Why" (e.g., comic books, adventure stories, etc.).

36. Teach new vocabulary words prior to having the student read the material.

37. Pair the student with a peer to summarize material in order to answer the questions "Who, What, Where, When, How and Why."

38. Have the student write and answer the questions "Who, What, Where, When, How and Why" using the Flash Card Study Aid. (See Appendix.)

1. Make certain the student is reading material on his/her ability level.

2. Modify or adjust reading materials to the student's ability level.

3. Set up a system of motivators, either tangible (e.g., extra computer time, helper for the day, etc.) or intangible (e.g., smile, handshake, praise, etc.) to encourage the student to be more successful in reading.

4. Tape record reading material for the student to listen to as he/she reads along.

5. Provide the student with a quiet place (e.g., carrel, study booth, "office," etc.) where he/she may go to engage in reading activities.

6. Write paragraphs and short stories for the student. These passages should be of high interest to the student using his/her name, family members, friends, pets, and interesting experiences.

7. Have the student dictate stories which are then written for him/her to read.

8. Have the student read high-interest signs, advertisements, notices, etc., from newspapers, magazines, movie promotions, etc.

9. Provide the student with many high-interest reading materials (e.g., comic books, magazines relating to sports or fashion, etc.).

10. Conduct a survey of the student's interests in order to provide reading material in that area.

11. Read, or have someone read, high-interest material to the student in order to promote his/her interest in reading.

12. Develop a library in the classroom that is appealing to the student (e.g., tent, bean bag chair, carpeted area, etc.).

13. Make reading materials easily accessible to the student in the classroom.

14. Provide the student with high-interest reading material that is also short in length in order that the student can finish reading the material without difficulty.

15. Encourage interest in reading by having students share interesting things they have read. This should be informal sharing in a group and not necessarily a "book report."

16. Have the student write to the author of material he/she reads in order to encourage an interest in reading more by the same author.

17. Encourage the student to read material with many illustrations and a limited amount of print. Gradually decrease the number of pictures.

18. Encourage parents to make reading material available to the student at home and to ensure that it is on the student's interest and reading level.

19. Encourage parents to read to their child at home and to have their child read to them. Encourage parents to read for their own enjoyment to serve as a model for their child.

20. Have the student read lower grade-level stories to younger children in order to enhance his/her feelings of confidence relative to reading.

21. Include predictable reading books in the class library. Predictability can make books more appealing to beginning readers and build confidence as well.

22. Avoid subjecting the student to uncomfortable reading situations (e.g., reading aloud in a group, identifying that the student's reading group is the lowest level, etc.).

23. Write periodic letters or notes to the student and encourage him/her to write back.

24. Set aside a fixed or random time (e.g., a half-hour daily, an hour a week, etc.) for a "Read-In." Everyone, teacher included, chooses a book that he/she likes and reads it for pleasure.

25. Expose the student to materials with large print. Large print can appear less intimidating to the student who does not choose to read.

26. Provide assistance in helping the student find reading material according to his/her interests and reading level. The student may not be comfortable or able to find books by himself/herself in the library.

27. Offer memberships in paperback book clubs to the student.

28. To encourage reading, make certain that the student knows he/she is not reading for assessment purposes but for enjoyment.

29. Make visiting the library an enjoyable weekly experience.

30. Encourage interesting reading by highlighting an author a month. The teacher should share information about an author, read books by the author and have additional titles by the author available for independent reading.

31. Pair the class with a lower grade-level class on a weekly basis in order for each student to read to a younger child.

32. Find a book series by an author that the student finds enjoyable. Make these books available for the student to read.

33. Read excerpts of your favorite children's books to entice the student to read the same book.

34. While teaching a unit in a content area, bring in related fiction or nonfiction books to share with your students to spark interest in reading.

1. Teach new vocabulary words and concepts prior to reading a selection.

2. Require the student to use new vocabulary words in follow-up assignments (e.g., have the student use these words on written assignments, crossword puzzles, etc.).

3. Have the student teach new vocabulary to his/her peers (e.g., require the student to be creative by showing, acting out, drawing or making an example of the word).

4. Teach the student to look for vocabulary words in italics, boldface, headings, and captions.

5. Teach the student to look for vocabulary definitions within the material read (e.g., The longhouse, **an Indian dwelling,** was used by Eastern Indians.).

6. Have the student list new or difficult words in categories such as people, food, animals, etc.

7. Have the student maintain a vocabulary notebook with definitions of words whose meanings he/she does not know.

8. When the student encounters a new word or one whose meaning he/she does not know, have the student practice making up sentences in which the word can be used in the correct context.

9. Have the student develop a picture dictionary in which he/she keeps those words which are difficult for him/her with a picture of the words or contextual clues.

10. Have the student identify a word a day he/she does not understand and require him/her to use that word throughout the day in various situations.

11. Have the student identify words he/she does not comprehend. Finding the definitions of these words can then become the student's dictionary assignment.

12. Have the student match vocabulary words with pictures representing the words.

13. Introduce new words and their meanings to the student before he/she reads new material.

14. Make certain the student learns the meanings of all commonly used prefixes and suffixes.

15. Make certain the student learns dictionary skills in order to be able to find meanings of words independently.

16. Identify a peer the student can rely upon to help him/her with the meanings of words not understood.

17. Provide the student with a variety of visual teaching materials to support word comprehension (e.g., filmstrips, pictures, charts, etc.).

18. Teach the student to use context clues to identify words he/she does not understand.

19. Label objects and activities in the classroom to help the student associate words with tangible aspects of his/her environment.

20. Have the student make a list of new words he/she has learned. The student can add words to the list at his/her own pace.

21. Reinforce the student for asking the meanings of words he/she does not understand.

22. Reinforce the student for looking up the definitions of words he/she does not understand.

23. Make it pleasant and positive for the student to ask the meanings or look up words he/she does not understand. Reinforce the student by assisting him/her, congratulating, praising, etc.

24. Make certain the student is developing a sight word vocabulary of the most commonly used words in his/her reading material.

25. Use a lower grade-level text as alternative reading material in subject areas.

26. Make certain the student underlines or circles words he/she does not understand. These words will become the student's vocabulary assignment for the next week.

27. Before reading, tell the student what he/she is to find in the story (e.g., who are the main characters, what are the main events, etc.).

28. Teach the student to predict what will happen in the story based on new vocabulary words and the title page.

29. Review new vocabulary words periodically with the student (e.g., weekly or bi-weekly).

30. Have the student review vocabulary words by providing related clues while the student deduces the vocabulary word.

31. Design classroom games (e.g., *Jeopardy, Pictionary*, etc.) to review vocabulary words periodically.

32. Prior to reading a selection, familiarize the student with the general content of the story to develop a point of reference. Through this approach, introduce new vocabulary words.

33. Teach the student synonyms and antonyms of familiar words to strengthen his/her vocabulary.

34. Outline reading material for the student using words and phrases on his/her reading level.

35. Make a list of main points from the student's reading material, written on the student's reading level.

36. Reduce distracting stimuli in order to increase the student's ability to concentrate on what he/she is reading (e.g., place the student on the front row, provide a carrel or "office" space away from distractions). This is used as a means of reducing distracting stimuli and not as a form of punishment.

37. Provide the student with a quiet place (e.g., carrel, study booth, etc.) where he/she may go to engage in reading activities.

38. Have the student outline, underline, or highlight important vocabulary in reading material.

39. Have the student read high-interest signs, advertisements, notices, etc., from newspapers, magazines, movie promotions, etc.; placing an emphasis on vocabulary skills.

77 Has difficulty applying decoding skills when reading

1. Teach the student a root word sight vocabulary in order to be able to add various prefixes and suffixes to develop word attack skills.

2. Obtain a list of words and phrases from the student's reading material which he/she does not recognize. Have the student practice phonics skills, context clues, structural analysis, etc., using these words.

3. Use a peer tutor to review word attack skills by utilizing games and activities.

4. Write paragraphs and short stories requiring decoding skills the student is currently learning. These passages should be of high interest to the student using his/her name, family members, friends, pets and interesting activities.

5. Have the student dictate stories which are then written for him/her to read, placing an emphasis on decoding skills.

6. Encourage the student to scan newspapers, magazines, etc., and underline words he/she can identify using decoding skills.

7. Teach the student the most common prefixes and suffixes to add to root words he/she can identify.

8. Teach the student to use context clues to identify words and phrases he/she does not know.

9. Develop a list of phonics sounds the student needs to master. Remove sounds from the list as the student demonstrates mastery of phonics skills.

10. Reinforce the student for using decoding skills when attempting to decode a word.

11. Have the student read high-interest signs, advertisements, notices, etc., from newspapers, magazines, movie promotions, etc.; placing an emphasis on decoding skills.

12. Make certain the student develops an awareness of seeing letter combinations that stand for a sound, prefix or suffix (e.g., have the student highlight all words in a reading passage that contain the suffix *-ed*).

13. Encourage the student to look for known sight words within a word to be decoded (e.g., for the word *interesting*, have the student identify the sight word *interest* to help decode the word).

14. Teach the student to be aware of word sounds and parts (e.g., read words with the /bl/ sound: blue, black, block, etc.).

15. Provide practice in reading a targeted group of words (e.g., words ending with *-ing*, etc.) by presenting a high-interest paragraph or story that contains these words.

16. Demonstrate skills in decoding words by modeling decoding words on the chalkboard or overhead (e.g., for the word *unassuming*, model decoding the word parts: *un-, -ing*, plus the root, to correctly read the word).

17. Encourage the student to try several sounds in order to arrive at the correct answer.

18. Have the student make a list of phonics skills he/she has mastered. The student continues to add to the list as he/she masters more and more skills.

19. Have the student identify syllables as he/she reads them in order to help him/her recognize word parts.

20. Encourage the student to learn additional basic sight words to assist him/her in reading.

21. Reduce the emphasis on competition. Competitive activities may cause the student to rush and not apply decoding skills accurately.

22. Provide the student with a list of common prefixes and suffixes to be posted on his/her desk to use as a reference when decoding words.

1. Create a list of words and phrases from the student's reading material which he/she does not recognize (e.g., have the science teacher identify the words the student will not recognize in the following week's assignment). These words and phrases will become the student's reading word list for the following week.

2. Modify or adjust reading materials to the student's ability level.

3. Outline reading material for the student using words and phrases on his/her reading level.

4. Teach the student to use context clues to identify words and phrases he/she does not know.

5. Emphasize that the student learn a root word sight vocabulary in order to be able to add various prefixes and suffixes, thus developing word attack skills.

6. Tape record difficult reading material for the student to listen to as he/she reads along.

7. Use a highlight marker to identify key words and phrases for the student. These words and phrases become the student's sight word vocabulary.

8. Teach the student to use related learning experiences in his/her classes (e.g., filmstrips, movies, tape recordings, demonstrations, discussions, videotapes, lectures, etc.). Encourage teachers to provide a variety of learning experiences for the student to enhance learning grade level sight words.

9. Use a sight word vocabulary approach in order to teach the student key words and phrases when reading directions and instructions (e.g., key words such as *circle, underline, match,* etc.).

10. Arrange for a peer tutor to practice sight words with the student to reinforce words learned.

11. Maintain mobility in order to be frequently near the student to provide reading assistance.

12. Use lower grade-level texts as alternative reading material in subject areas.

13. Write paragraphs and short stories using words the student is currently developing. These passages should be of high interest to the student using his/her name, family members, friends, pets, and interesting experiences.

14. Have the student dictate stories which are then written for him/her to read, placing an emphasis on reading skills.

15. Have the student read high-interest signs, advertisements, notices, etc., from newspapers, movie promotions, magazines, etc.; placing an emphasis on reading skills.

16. Make certain the student is practicing reading skills which are directly related to high-interest reading activities (e.g., adventures, romance, mystery, athletics, etc.).

17. Reduce the emphasis on competition. Competitive activities may cause the student to hurry and make errors.

18. Provide the student with computer software to practice sight words he/she is learning. Drill and repetition is often necessary to commit words to memory.

19. Teach the student to use context clues to identify sight words the student is learning.

20. Provide the student with a quiet area (e.g., carrel, study booth, etc.) where he/she may go to practice sight words.

21. Provide the student with many high-interest reading materials (e.g., comic books, magazines, etc.) to practice sight words.

22. Encourage the student to read material with many illustrations and context clues to support learning new sight words.

79 Cannot summarize/retell important concepts after reading a selection

1. Teach the student to recognize main points, important facts, etc., by answering "Who, What, Where, When, How, and Why." (See Appendix for the Outline Form.)

2. Make certain the student is reading material on his/her level.

3. Modify or adjust reading material to the student's ability level.

4. Read shorter selections with the student, discussing the story in a one-on-one situation. Gradually increase the length of selections as the student demonstrates success.

5. Tape record reading material for the student to listen to as he/she reads along. Have the student stop at various points to retell/summarize the selection.

6. After reading a short story, have the student identify the main characters, sequence the events, and report the outcome of the story.

7. Relate the information being read to the student's previous experiences.

8. Assess the meaningfulness of the material being read to the student. Comprehension is more likely to occur when the material is meaningful and the student can relate to real experiences.

9. Have the student verbally paraphrase material he/she has read in order to assess his/her comprehension.

10. Prior to reading a selection, prepare an outline for the student to refer to and add details to while reading the selection.

11. Make a list of main points from the student's reading material. Have the student discuss each main point after reading the selection.

12. Teach the student to identify main points in material he/she has read in order to assess his/her comprehension.

13. Have the student outline, underline or highlight important points in reading material.

14. Have the student take notes while he/she is reading in order to increase comprehension.

15. Underline or highlight important points **before** the student reads the selection.

16. Give the student sufficient time to read a selection, emphasizing comprehension not speed.

17. Teach the student to think about the selection and predict what will happen next, prior to completing the selection.

18. Teach the student to look for key concepts when reading a selection.

19. Teach the student when reading a selection to look for key words and main ideas that answer "Who, What, Where, When, How, and Why."

20. Have the student read independently each day to practice reading skills.

21. Teach new vocabulary words prior to having the student read the material.

22. Have the student answer in writing the questions "Who, What, Where, When, How, and Why" using a Flash Card Study Aid. (See Appendix.)

23. After reading a selection, have the student complete a semantic map answering the questions "Who, What, Where, When, How, and Why." (See Appendix for Mapping Form.)

24. Arrange for a peer tutor to read with the student to develop comprehension skills.

25. Prior to reading a selection, familiarize the student with the general context of the story. (e.g., if the selection is about elephants, brainstorm and discuss elephants to develop a point of reference).

26. When reading orally with the student, pause at various points to discuss material read up to that point. Have the student predict what will happen next before proceeding.

27. Have the student complete a Fiction Frame after reading a selection. (See Appendix.)

28. Require the student to read a selection more than once, emphasizing comprehension rather than speed.

29. Teach the student to look for story elements when reading a selection (e.g., setting, characters, plot, ending). (See Appendix for Fiction Frame.)

1. Make certain the student is reading material on his/her level.

2. Highlight or underline those words the student most frequently fails to recognize in different contexts.

3. Use a lower grade-level text as alternative reading material in subject areas.

4. Write paragraphs and short stories using those words the student most frequently fails to recognize in different contexts. These paragraphs should be of high interest to the student using his/her name, family members, friends, pets, and interesting experiences.

5. Make a reading "window" for the student. The student moves the reading "window" across and down the page as he/she reads.

6. Have the student list those words he/she most frequently fails to recognize into categories such as people, food, animals, etc., in order to help the student recognize those words in different contexts.

7. Teach the student to use context clues to identify words he/she does not understand.

8. Identify words the student does not recognize in different contexts and put these words on flash cards. Have the student match these words to the same words in sentences, paragraphs, short stories, etc.

9. Have the student print/write those words he/she most frequently fails to recognize in different contexts.

10. Have the student maintain a list with definitions of those words he/she most frequently fails to recognize in different contexts.

11. Highlight or underline those words in reading material the student is unable to recognize. Have the student identify those words as he/she reads them.

12. Reduce distracting stimuli in order to increase the student's ability to concentrate on what he/she is reading (e.g., place the student on the front row, provide a carrel or "office" space away from distractions). This is used as a means of reducing distracting stimuli and not as a form of punishment.

13. Provide the student with a quiet place (e.g., carrel, study booth, etc.) where he/she may go to engage in reading activities.

14. Reduce the emphasis on competition. Competitive activities may cause the student to hurry and fail to recognize words in a particular context.

15. Provide the student with a dictionary and require him/her to find the definitions of those words he/she does not recognize.

16. Have the student read short sentences in order to make it easier to recognize words in different contexts. Longer sentences are presented as the student demonstrates success.

17. Provide the student with large print reading material in order to increase the likelihood of the student recognizing words in different contexts.

IV. APPENDIX

Note Taking

1. For note taking from lecture or written material, follow:

    ● **Outline Form**
      (e.g., Who, What, Where, When, How, Why)

    ● **Mapping Form**
      (e.g., Who, What, Where, When, How, Why)

    ● **Double-Column Form**
      (e.g., Who, What, Where, When, How, Why)

2. For note taking from directions, follow:

    ● **Assignment Form**
      (e.g., What, How, Materials, When)

    ● **Assignment Sheet**

    ● **2-Week Project Outline**

Outline Form

SUBJECT: _____

      Topic: _____

	General	**Specific**
Who:		
What:		
Where:		
When:		
How:		
Why:		
Vocabulary:		

Outline Form (Alternative)

SUBJECT: _____

Topic: _____

General   Specific

What:

Why:

How:

Vocabulary:

Example:

Mapping Form

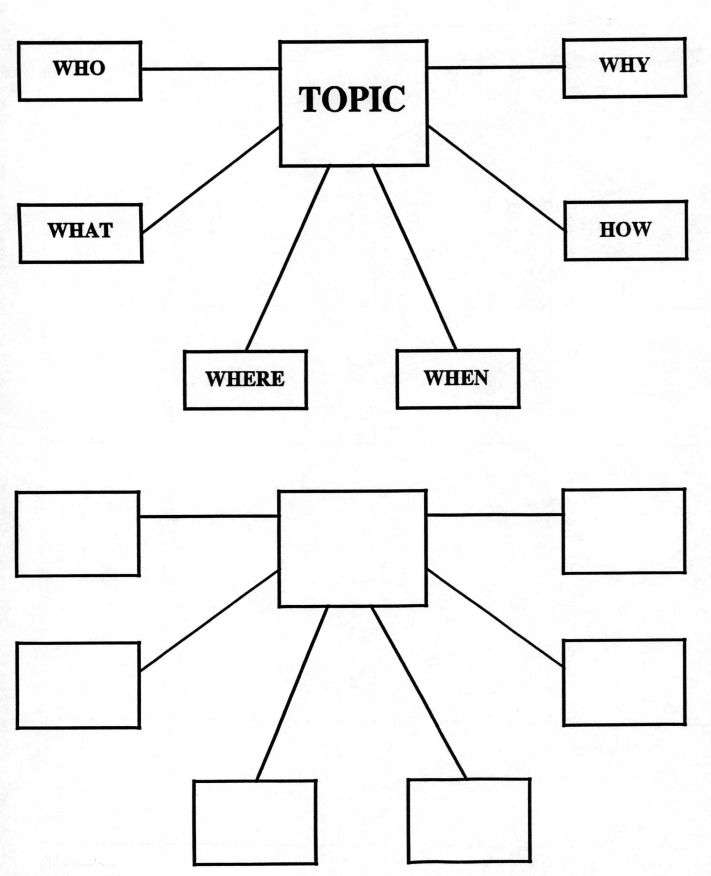

Double-Column Form

Who

What

Where

When

How

Why

Assignment Form

Subject:_____

	General	Specific
What:		
How:		
Materials:		
When:		

Subject:_____

	General	Specific
What:		
How:		
Materials:		
When:		

Assignment Sheet

ASSIGNMENT SHEET   DATE _____

SUBJECT	ASSIGNMENT	DUE DATE	TEACHER SIGNATURE
Math			
Reading			
Science			
Social Studies			
Spelling			
Other			

_____   Comments:

PARENT SIGNATURE

ASSIGNMENT SHEET   DATE _____

SUBJECT	ASSIGNMENT	DUE DATE	TEACHER SIGNATURE
Math			
History			
Science			
English			
Fine Arts/ Practical Arts			
Other			

_____   Comments:

PARENT SIGNATURE

2-Week Project Outline

DAY 1   **Determine exactly what the assignment is**
- **Identify due date**

DAY 2-4   **Project Preparation**
- **READ ASSIGNED MATERIALS**
- **RESEARCH RELATED MATERIALS**
- **GATHER NECESSARY MATERIALS**

DAY 5   **Summarize reading material by answering:**
- **Who, What, Where, When, How, Why**

DAY 6   **Preliminary project construction**
- **Make sketches, determine scale, make revisions**

DAY 7-11   **Project construction**
- **Lay out all materials**
- **Prepare materials to scale**
- **Draw/color**
- **Cut**
- **Glue**
- **Paint**

DAY 12   **Touch up work**
- **Label, check that all items are secure, etc.**

DAY 13   **Write paragraph from summary (Day 5)**

DAY 14   **Turn in!**

Test-Taking Skills

1. Survey entire test for the kinds of items that are included (e.g., true-false, multiple-choice, fill-in-the-blank, etc.).

2. Read all directions.

3. Underline or circle all key words in directions (e.g., locate, write, choose the best answer, identify the main idea, etc.).

4. Do not answer any items until the directions are thoroughly understood (i.e., ask the teacher for clarification if directions are not thoroughly understood).

5. Respond to all items for which the answer is known, skipping remaining items to answer later (some items may provide clues or reminders for items the student could not answer the first time through the test).

6. For those items which are difficult to answer, underline the key words (e.g., who, what, where, when, how, why) and then respond.

7. For those items still not understood, ask the teacher for clarification.

8. Go back and check all answers for accuracy (e.g., followed directions, proper use of math operations, no careless errors).

ADDITIONAL SUGGESTIONS

- In order for a statement to be true, all of the statement must be true (e.g., note words such as *all, never, always, etc.*).

- When matching, first answer items that are known, crossing off answers that are used, then go back to remaining items and make the best choice.

- Some items may provide clues or reminders for items the student could not answer the first time through the test.

- When writing an essay answer, construct the answer around Who, What, Where, When, How, and Why.

- On multiple-choice items, read all choices before responding. If any of the choices look new or different, they are probably not the correct answer.

- If a true-false item looks new or different, it is probably false.

Studying for a Test

1. Identify the information to be covered on the test.

2. Identify and collect all necessary materials (e.g., textbook, notebook, etc.).

3. Identify major topics.

4. Under each topic identify major headings.

5. Under each heading identify Who, What, Where, When, How, and Why.

6. Write this information on the Outline Form
         or
   underline this information
         or
   highlight this information.

7. Make study aids such as flash cards. (See Appendix.)

8. Memorize information using the Outline Form and/or mnemonic devices

ADDITIONAL SUGGESTIONS

● Study with a friend.

● Write practice questions from the Outline Form and answer the questions.

● If study questions are provided, answer all questions.

● Make certain that all information in the summary is thoroughly understood.

Flash Card Study Aid

Questions   **Topic:** _____

Who:

What:

Where:

When:

How:

Why:

Topic: _____

Who:

What:

Where:

When:

How:

Why:

Fiction Frame

TITLE: _____

AUTHOR: _____

This story takes place _____. An important character in this story

is _____ who _____.

A problem occurs when _____

_____.

Next, _____

_____.

The problem is solved when _____

_____

_____.

At the end of the story, _____

_____

_____.

Parent Letter Sample

Dear Parents:

Your child will be bringing home an assignment sheet daily. This assignment sheet will indicate the assignments that are to be completed at home and when they are due.

Please check for this sheet every day in order to monitor homework completion. After all assignments are complete, please sign the sheet and return it to school with your child. Thank you for your support.

Sincerely,

Selected Abbreviations and Symbols

ab.	about		$	money
add.	addition		mo.	month
&	and		natl.	national
bk.	book		no.	number
bldg.	building		#	number
cap.	capital		oz.	ounce
c/o	care of		p., pg.	page
cm.	centimeter		pd.	paid
cent.	century		par.	paragraph
ch., chap.	chapter		pop.	population
co.	company		lb.	pound
cont.	continent		pres.	president
cont.	continued		qt.	quart
corp.	corporation		rd.	road
dept.	department		rep.	representative
dict.	dictionary		Rev.	Reverend
educ.	education		sch.	school
enc.	encyclopedia		sc.	science
Eng.	English		sig.	signature
fig.	figure		s.s.	social studies
geog.	geography		sp.	spelling
govt.	government		sq.	square
gr.	gram		subj.	subject
ht.	height		subt.	subtraction
hist.	history		syn.	synonym
ill., illus.	illustration		temp.	temperature
in.	inch		t.	ton
intro.	introduction		treas.	treasurer
lab.	laboratory		U.S.A.	United States of America
lang.	language		univ.	university
lat.	latitude		v.	verb
leg.	legislature		vs.	versus
lib.	library		v.p.	vice-president
liq.	liquid		wk.	week
max.	maximum		wt.	weight
meas.	measure		w/	with
mi.	mile		yd.	yard
min.	minute		yr.	year
misc.	miscellaneous			

The above list only serves as an example. The student should further develop his/her own list.

Typical Methods of Modifying Academic Tasks

- Reduce the number of problems on a page (e.g., five problems to a page; the student may be required to do four pages of work throughout the day if necessary).

- Use a highlight marker to identify key words, phrases, or sentences for the student to read.

- Remove pages from workbooks or reading material and present these to the student one at a time rather than allowing the student to become anxious with workbooks or texts.

- Outline reading material for the student at his/her reading level, emphasizing main ideas.

- Tape record material for the student to listen to as he/she reads along.

- Read tests/quizzes aloud for the student.

- Tape record tests/quizzes for the student.

- Make a bright construction paper border for the student to place around reading material in order to maintain his/her attention to the task.

- Make a reading window from construction paper which the student places over sentences or paragraphs in order to maintain attention.

- Provide manipulative objects for the student to use in solving math problems.

- Rearrange problems on a page (e.g., if crowded, create more space between the problems).

- Use graph paper for math problems, handwriting, etc.

- Rewrite directions at a more appropriate reading level.

- Tape record directions.

- Have peers deliver directions or explanations.

- Allow more time to take tests or quizzes.

Preventing Behavior Problems

- Determine reinforcer preferences

- Determine academic ability levels

- Determine social interaction skills

- Determine ability to remain on task

- Determine group behavior

- Monitor and limit contemporary determinants of inappropriate behavior such as having to wait, task length, task difficulty, peer involvement, etc.

- Base seating arrangements on behavior

- Base group involvement on behavior

- Maintain teacher mobility in classroom

- Maintain teacher/student contact: visual, verbal, and physical

- Use criteria for expectations based on observed behavior and performance

- Use shaping, fading, and imitation procedures to gradually change behavior

- Maintain variety in reinforcers

- Use the Premack Principle in arranging schedule (i.e., a more desirable behavior can be used to reinforce the completion of a less desirable behavior)

- Use curriculum as reinforcement

- Use rules, point cards, and schedules of daily events as discriminative stimuli

- Use contracting to individualize, specify expected behavior, and identify reinforcers

- Arrange seating so all students have visibility to and from the teacher and teacher can scan the entire class

- Maintain a full schedule of activities

- Use language that is positive and firm, not demeaning, insulting, or harassing

- Intervene early when any form of conflict occurs

- Do not ignore behavior as an excuse for not intervening

- Use time-out to help the student resolve problem behavior

- Use removal to prevent contagion, destruction of property, and danger to others

- Communicate and coordinate with other teachers

- Communicate with home to prevent students playing one adult against another

Reinforcer Survey

Name: _____ Age: _____

Date: _____

1. The things I like to do after school are _____
   _____

2. If I had ten dollars I would _____
   _____

3. My favorite TV programs are _____
   _____

4. My favorite game at school is _____
   _____

5. My best friends are _____

6. My favorite time of day is _____
   _____

7. My favorite toys are _____

8. My favorite record is _____

9. My favorite subject at school is _____
   _____

10. I like to read books about _____
    _____

11. The places I like to go in town are _____
    _____

12. My favorite foods are _____
    _____

13. My favorite inside activities are _____
    _____

14. My favorite outside activities are _____
    _____

15. My hobbies are _____
    _____

16. My favorite animals are _____
    _____

17. The three things I like to do most are _____
    _____

The Reinforcer Survey may be given to one student or a group of students. If the students cannot read, the survey is read to them. If they cannot write their answers, the answers are given verbally.

A List of Reinforcers Identified by Elementary-Aged Students

1. Listen to the radio
2. Free time
3. Watch favorite program on TV
4. Talk to best friend
5. Listen to favorite tapes
6. Read a book
7. Candy, especially chocolate
8. Play sports - baseball, kickball, soccer, hockey
9. Ride a bike
10. Do something fun with best friend
11. Go to the zoo
12. Build a model plane or car
13. Go to the arcade and play video games
14. Camping trip
15. Play with pets
16. Go to a fast-food restaurant
17. Pop popcorn
18. Go to a movie
19. Play in the gym
20. Play outside
21. Help clean up classroom
22. Play with puppets
23. Play with dolls and a doll house
24. Ice cream
25. Cookies
26. Go shopping at a grocery store
27. Tacos
28. Hamburgers and french fries
29. Pizza
30. Money
31. Making buttons
32. Parties
33. Teacher's helper
34. Field trips
35. Eat lunch outside on a nice day
36. Recess
37. Student-of-the-month
38. Honor roll
39. Buy sodas
40. Work on puzzles
41. Write on the chalkboard
42. Gumball machine
43. Race cars
44. Use colored markers
45. Roller skating
46. Puppet show
47. Water slide
48. Stickers
49. Pencils
50. Use the computer
51. Fly model airplanes
52. Visit the principal

A List of Reinforcers Identified by Secondary-Aged Students

1. Free time

   - Doing nothing

   - Reading magazines (from home or library)

   - Reading newspapers

   - Writing a letter (to a rock star, favorite author, politician, probation officer, friend)

   - Peer tutoring (your class or another one)

   - Listen to records (from class, library, home)

   - Visit library

   - Work on a hobby

   - See a film

   - Draw - Paint - Create

2. Acting as teacher assistant (any length of time)

3. Acting as principal assistant (any length of time)

4. Have class outside

5. Field trip

6. Go to a movie

7. Have a soda

8. Have an afternoon for a sport activity (some students play and some watch)

9. Play a game (Bingo, cards, board games)

10. Use a camera (take pictures and have them developed)

11. Play Trivia games

12. Time off from school

13. Coach's assistant (any length of time)

14. Picnic lunch

15. Run errands

16. Extra time in high interest areas (shop, art, P.E.)

17. Do clerical work in building (use copy machine, run office errands)

18. Library assistant (any length of time)

19. Custodian's assistant (any length of time)

20. Watch TV

21. Earn a model

22. Typing

23. Attend a sports event

24. Food or treat coupons

25. Iron-on decals

Reinforcer Menu

REINFORCER MENU

Reinforcer	Points Needed
Working with Clay	30
Peer Tutoring	25
Using Colored Markers	30
Using Colored Chalk	30
Feeding Pets	20
Delivering Messages	15
Carrying Wastebasket	20
Operating Projector	30
Playing a Board Game	35
Leading the Class Line	25
Passing out Materials	20
Using a Typewriter	25
Trip to Library	25

CLASS REINFORCER MENU

Reinforcer	Points Needed
See a Film	30
Class Visitor	25
Write and Mail Letters	30
Field Trip	30
Lunch Outdoors	20
Pop Popcorn	35
Take Class Pictures	30
Tape Songs	15
Put on a Play	25
Have Adults in for Lunch	30
Work with a Peer All Day	25

The Reinforcer Menu is compiled from information gathered by having a student or students respond to the Reinforcer Survey.

Point Card

TIME	DAYS OF WEEK				
	M	T	W	T	F
8:00 - 8:50					
9:00 - 9:50					
10:00 - 10:50					
11:00 - 11:30					
11:30 - 12:20					
12:30 - 1:20					
1:30 - 2:20					
2:30 - 3:20					

Name: _____

This is a Point Card for secondary level students and may be used in special education classes or in regular classes. Teachers assign points, give checks, or sign initials for appropriate behavior demonstrated by the student while in the classroom. These points are relative to rules of the classroom, expected behavior, a contract developed with the student, etc. The card is a 3 x 5 inch index card which is easily kept in a shirt pocket and is small enough to reduce embarrassment for some students who would prefer to keep their behavioral support program more confidential.

Point Record

ACADEMIC POINTS

Monday | 1 | 2 | 3 | 4 | 5 | 6 | 7 | 8 | 9 | 10 | 11 | 12 | 13 | 14

Tuesday | 1 | 2 | 3 | 4 | 5 | 6 | 7 | 8 | 9 | 10 | 11 | 12 | 13 | 14

Wednesday | 1 | 2 | 3 | 4 | 5 | 6 | 7 | 8 | 9 | 10 | 11 | 12 | 13 | 14

Thursday | 1 | 2 | 3 | 4 | 5 | 6 | 7 | 8 | 9 | 10 | 11 | 12 | 13 | 14

Friday | 1 | 2 | 3 | 4 | 5 | 6 | 7 | 8 | 9 | 10 | 11 | 12 | 13 | 14

SOCIAL POINTS

Monday

Tuesday

Wednesday

Thursday

Friday

The Point Record form provides for Academic Points, top section, for each task completed with criteria met; and Social Points, bottom section, for demonstrating appropriate behavior in and around the classroom. The Point Record is kept with the student at all times, wherever he/she may be, in order that points may be given for following any school rules.

Rules For School Environments

GENERAL SOCIAL RULES....

- BE QUIET
- REMAIN IN YOUR SEAT
- WORK ON ASSIGNED TASK
- RAISE YOUR HAND

HALLWAY RULES....

- WALK IN THE HALL
- WALK IN A LINE
- WALK ON THE RIGHT
- WALK QUIETLY

CAFETERIA RULES....

- BE QUIET IN THE CAFETERIA LINE
- WALK TO YOUR TABLE
- TALK QUIETLY
- REMAIN SEATED

OUTDOOR RULES....

- TAKE PART IN SOME ACTIVITY
- TAKE TURNS
- BE FRIENDLY
- LINE UP WHEN IT IS TIME

ACADEMIC RULES....

- FINISH ONE TASK
- MEET YOUR CRITERIA
  TO EARN 5 POINTS

These rules, except for perhaps the outdoor rules, are applicable to all grade levels and have been used in public schools for general behavioral expectations.

Student Conference Report

Student's Name: _____

School Personnel Involved and Titles: _____

_____

Date: _____ Grade Level of Student: _____

. . . .

Initiation of Conference: Regularly Scheduled Conference _____

Teacher Initiation _____ Other Personnel Initiation _____

Student Initiation _____ Parent Initiation _____

. . . .

Nature of Communication: Information Sharing _____

Progress Update _____ Problem Identification _____

Other _____

. . . .

Conference Summary (Copies of Written Communication Should Be Attached): _____

_____

_____

_____

_____

_____

_____

. . . .

Expectations Based on Conference: _____

_____

_____

. . . .

Signatures of Conference Participants: _____

_____

_____

. . . .

The Student Conference Report is a record of conferences held with the student to identify problems, concerns, progress, etc.

Parent Communication Form

Teacher: _____ Date: _____ Grade or Level:_____

Parent(s): _____ Student: _____ Type of Class: _____

Other School Personnel: _____

. . . .

TYPE OF COMMMUNICATION: Letter _____ Note _____ Telephone _____

Parent Visit to School _____ Teacher Visit to Home _____

Out-of-School Location _____ Other _____

. . . .

Initiation of Communication: School Scheduled Meeting _____

Teacher Initiation _____ Parent Initiation _____ Other _____

. . . .

Nature of Communication: Information Sharing _____Progress Update _____ Problem Identification _____ Other_____
. . . .

Communication Summary (Copies of Written Communications Should Be Attached):
_____

_____

_____

_____

_____

. . . .

Expectations for Further Communication: _____

_____

_____

. . . .

Signatures of Participants (If Communication Made in Person): _____

_____

_____

The Parent Communication Form is used to document communication made with parents in person, by telephone, or by notes or letters.

Schedule of Daily Events

SCHEDULE OF DAILY EVENTS

NAME _____

	#1	#2	#3	#4	#5	#6	#7	#8	#9	#10
Monday										
Tuesday										
Wednesday										
Thursday										
Friday										

SCHEDULE OF DAILY EVENTS

NAME _____

	#1	#2	#3	#4	#5	#6	#7	#8	#9	#10
Tuesday										

Each individual student's Schedule of Daily Events is developed for him/her and attached to his/her desk for a week at a time or for one day at a time. This schedule identifies each activity/task the student is assigned for the day, and the schedule is filled in by the teacher one day at a time. Students tend to know what they are to do next when the schedule is provided, and teachers can expect fewer interruptions for directions when students refer to their schedules.

V. Index